GOING UNDERGROUND THE BLACK COUNTRY

ANTHONY POULTON-SMITH

AMBERLEY

Front cover image courtesy of Dudley Archives and Local History Service.

First published 2024

Amberley Publishing, The Hill, Stroud
Gloucestershire GL5 4EP

www.amberley-books.com

British Library Cataloguing in Publication Data.
A catalogue record for this book is available from the British Library.

ISBN 978 1 3981 1622 1 (print)
ISBN 978 1 3981 1623 8 (ebook)

Typesetting by Hurix Digital, India.
Printed in the UK.

CONTENTS

1

BENEATH OUR FEET

The Black Country is a region of the Midlands covering an area of almost 140 square miles with a population approaching 1.2 million, so it seems odd to discover that it has no settled borders. It is so named either for the smoke pouring from countless chimneys from forges and foundries during the Industrial Revolution and/or the large seams of coal mined in the area to feed those fires. In the twenty-first century, however, the region is more rural than many envisage.

Today, the major artery through the Black Country, the M5 motorway, runs not just above ground but is also elevated through much of its route here. Before the internal-combustion engine became the normal mode of travel, railways and the earlier canal network crossed the region, and several of these routes included running below ground in purpose-built tunnels. Many of these still exist: some still carry passengers beneath the region while others lie abandoned and sealed away from the modern world.

We must also remember the mining, particularly that of coal, which enabled industry to make this a stronghold in these islands. Many of those workings are still to be found, an echo of the days before the seams were worked out. Clay, ironstone, limestone, and stone for building has also been extracted on an industrial scale over the centuries. There have also been natural underground features; caves have been utilised for storage and as homes, as we shall see.

Like many regions where humans have resided for millennia, something of those early times lies buried. Much of this area has been important since at least the Saxon era, as the very place names attest. While growth only came with the Industrial Revolution, that expansion proved explosive as those who worked the land flooded into the area to learn the new skills required in taking newly created industries.

Very few of us will have seen what exists beneath our feet. Likely the most we ever see is when peering into the hole in the street as workmen perform maintenance on telephone, cable, power lines, gas and water pipes, or sewerage. Travelling on the railways and canals of yesteryear reveals little, even with a powerful light source, and spatial awareness of just what lies around the tunnel is impossible to grasp. Yet all we require is to see that hole as a cross-section, instead of from above, for us to realise the surprising amount beneath our streets.

Doubtless the most readily seen are the drains – metal grilles along the gutters taking water away from the surface. Being open to the sky by necessity – it's where the water comes from! – it is the most familiar sight for us. But we only see a small opening and little of what lies beneath, or how deep that run-off gets. Yet legislation clearly defines what we are unable to see, the minimum and maximum depths of drainage systems being 75 cm and 135 cm below finished ground level, respectively. Such depths below the made road level (note, not the natural ground level) are not chosen arbitrarily. Frost should not prove a problem at the minimum depth of 75 cm – although location and altitude can alter these expectations significantly – while a maximum of 135 cm will allow access for maintenance and repairs.

Yet that is not the whole story, for these features allow the water to drain away in three ways. Initially the drop is quite shallow, for what is not wanted is to find this water flooding into the sewers where the so-called foul water awaits treatment. A shallow run-off will allow, in the case of isolated small numbers of properties, the surface water to be sent to a nearby soakaway. As the area becomes more built up, and therefore more water running off the man-made roads, a dedicated surface water sewer (often known as a stormwater drain) likely takes this volume to a nearby watercourse. Lastly the water can, under certain conditions, be directed to the sewer with the foul water, although this does increase the volume requiring treatment, putting a strain on the sewage treatment processes. Note it is technically wrong to refer to a sewer as such when it only serves one property, then it is officially a drain. Such can only cause confusion, when a sewer can sometimes be a drain and vice versa, and that is before the complexity of sewerage laws are taken into consideration.

Having mentioned sewage, we should also view the different methods employed to move this undesirable content along and where it ends up. Again, remote locations are the simplest, for these properties will utilise a septic tank or sludge tank. However, as most will know, the vast majority is taken to sewage farms for treatment. This process separates out the clean water, which is diverted to the river system, and recyclable organic products, with the latter used as fertilisers. Unfortunately, many other items find their way into the sewers, be they washed down drains after being discarded thoughtlessly instead of using waste bins, or wrongly flushed down a toilet. There are very good reasons why we are told not to put oil-based products down a drain and not to flush anything other than toilet paper.

Movement of sewage is an early technology and thus uses the simplest means: gravity and liquid. Next time you feel breathless after ascending that steep hill, take a breath at the top and look back down the slope. Remember, everything underground must also negotiate that hill, albeit in the case of sewers running the opposite way to your ascent. Imagine what would happen if the load of sewage in that drop was allowed to cascade the whole length of the drop unrestricted. It would gather at the foot and the whole system would soon be blocked. Thus, steps are incorporated to create a series of waterfalls, bringing the contents to the base in a manageable volume. Such is the simplicity of the system that little can go wrong with it. Hence, if you see the road dug up for sewer repair, it is likely the problem is improper use of the system. And if you think a small item flushed could not possibly cause a problem, think again.

Undoubtedly the biggest problem in modern sewage systems is the dreaded 'fatberg'. The clumps of non-biodegradable matter (which covers anything that should not be in the sewer) build up to such a size they can easily cause blockages. In London in 2018 a fatberg was discovered in a sewer comprised of congealed fat from kitchens, wet wipes, disposable nappies, oil, condoms and feminine hygiene products. It took nine weeks to clear just 130 metres of sewer by the removal of a toxic monster weighing in at an astonishing 250 tonnes.

These statistics alone give a clue as to the size of what is to be found beneath our feet, although most of our town's sewers are rather smaller than those in the capital. While they can be shallower than we would think, sewage pipes will always be at least 2 metres beneath the surface to prevent freezing temperatures proving problematic. A frozen river of biodegradable matter, together with the associated odours, would soon cause appalling problems for the world above. When chums pointed out the 'stinkpipes' or 'stenchpoles' on the road to school, they would explain this was to rid the subterranean world of its unpleasant odours. These stories were partially correct, for they were linked to the sewers but were designed to permit the escape of methane, a potentially explosive gas, and a natural byproduct of the decomposition process.

Underground pipes do not only allow the passage of water and sewage. Today it is not unusual to find a house claiming it is all-electric, and yet it was only a century ago that many homes had no electricity supply and were powered entirely by gas. Gas fed to the properties in underground pipes, with supplies to individual properties coming in pipes feeding off the gas main coming along the street. Legislation also controls gas pipes, each required to be a minimum 75 cm under a road or verge, although only 60 cm under a footpath. Coming off the main, service pipes to residential properties should be a minimum of 37.5 cm on private ground and 45 cm under footpaths and highways.

Anyone taking the time to stand alongside an excavated hole, will realise the gas main is rather more than 75 cm below the surface. The same is true of water and sewage pipes, which are normally much older than the cables of electricity, television, and internet. This is not because previous generations buried their pipes deeper, either by choice or legislation, the truth is the street level has risen over years. It is quite natural to build on top of earlier constructions and, as archaeologists will tell us, the deeper one digs, the further back in time one gets.

Electricity supplies came to parts of the Black Country in 1895, when Wolverhampton became connected, Walsall saw the electric light in 1916, with others connected by a century ago. Cables were required to be buried a minimum of 60 cm under roads and pavements, then under driveways this rose to 45 cm, but under soil and grass on 15 cm (rather less than a spade's depth), and just 10 cm beneath concrete or paving on the property. Note today the recommended depth for electricity cables under flowerbeds is given as two spade depths, although this is merely a guideline, not a requirement. Cables, including those of cable television and internet services, these little more than a generation old, are much easier to damage than pipes and are enclosed in conduit for added protection, and are colour coded, using coloured tape with warning marks, and similar messages to identify the contents without having to sever same. With this network of pipes and cables beneath our towns, bringing services we tend to take for granted, it is surprising we do not see the roads dug up more often. Do we ever consider what lies beneath the roads and pavements until workmen put up barriers around a new hole?

Our towns and villages also have basements, both modern and old, used and abandoned, hidden, forgotten and even, on occasions, still utilised. Furthermore, we should also acknowledge the archaeology. While not technically accessible, which probably prevents any suggestion they are 'underground' and should be considered 'buried', they do warrant at least a brief look.

Many will know the towns making up the Black Country: Sandwell, West Bromwich, Oldbury, Blackheath, Cradley Heath, Old Hill, Bilston, Dudley, Tipton, Wednesfield, Halesowen, Wednesbury, Walsall, Wolverhampton, Smethwick, and Stourbridge. Although few will agree on which towns (or even specific areas within those towns) are in or outside the Black Country, for the purposes of this book all those towns and areas between are considered relevant. In the following pages something of the hidden world beneath the ground will be revealed and all manner of surprising discoveries unearthed – some well-known or predictable, others long buried, forgotten or previously unknown.

2

KINVER HOLY AUSTIN ROCK HOUSES

At 269 metres above sea level, Turners Hill is the highest point in the Black Country. Among the next highest points is Kinver Holy Austin Ridge. In a book looking at what lies under the ground it might seem odd to begin looking up to 164 metres above sea level, yet here we find the Holy Austin rock houses. Known as 'Holy Austin' as it was home to a hermit until the Reformation, the rock houses provided homes to families from at least the early seventeenth century.

This sandstone ridge is easily carved, be it naturally, through erosion, or by the hand of man. The latter is certainly how local families carved out an existence until as recently as the 1960s, when Vale's Rock (also known as Crow's Rock) was a home of two levels. Its dangerous condition has seen the area fenced off today as erosion has made this part very unsafe. The earliest known reference to example of a family resident at Kinver Edge rock houses is at Nanny's Rock. Here a large cavern with no less than five compartments exists and, while there is no official record of a resident family, it seems likely this cavern is also the 'Meg-o-Fox-Hole' as referred to as home to 'Margaret of the Fox Earth' from the burial record of 8 June 1617.

These are not the only caves in this area. Mill Lane boasts smaller caves, once storage areas for the now-demolished houses that stood here, while opposite the Staffordshire and Worcestershire Canal in the region known as Gibraltar there are more extensive caverns. All these rock houses were enlarged from the original caverns, with additions to make comfortable and spacious living accommodations. These additions would be seen as necessities to us, for these were doors, windows, and chimney flues, even to the point of using stone, brick, and tile, as well as wood and glass, to create same. Those chimneys and flues allowed fireplaces to warm the interiors, with these constructed around the edge of the rockface. Inside, natural niches provided storage opportunities, as did the shelves added to the walls. These are where kitchenware and personal items would be displayed, with pictures and photographs on the walls.

There is also evidence of holes in the walls where floor joists were placed to support an upper floor. These homes came with ready-made walls, roofs, and ceilings. Remember, though, these were of sandstone. This rock not only erodes readily but, more importantly, is highly porous, and water seeping in would have proved a constant concern. We should not imagine the walls were the red of the bare rock. Some were certainly plastered and, as a minimum, limewashed. With contemporary furniture of table and chairs, brass bedsteads, cushions, rugs, mats, etc., it is nearly impossible to tell these unique homes from a contemporary indoor photograph.

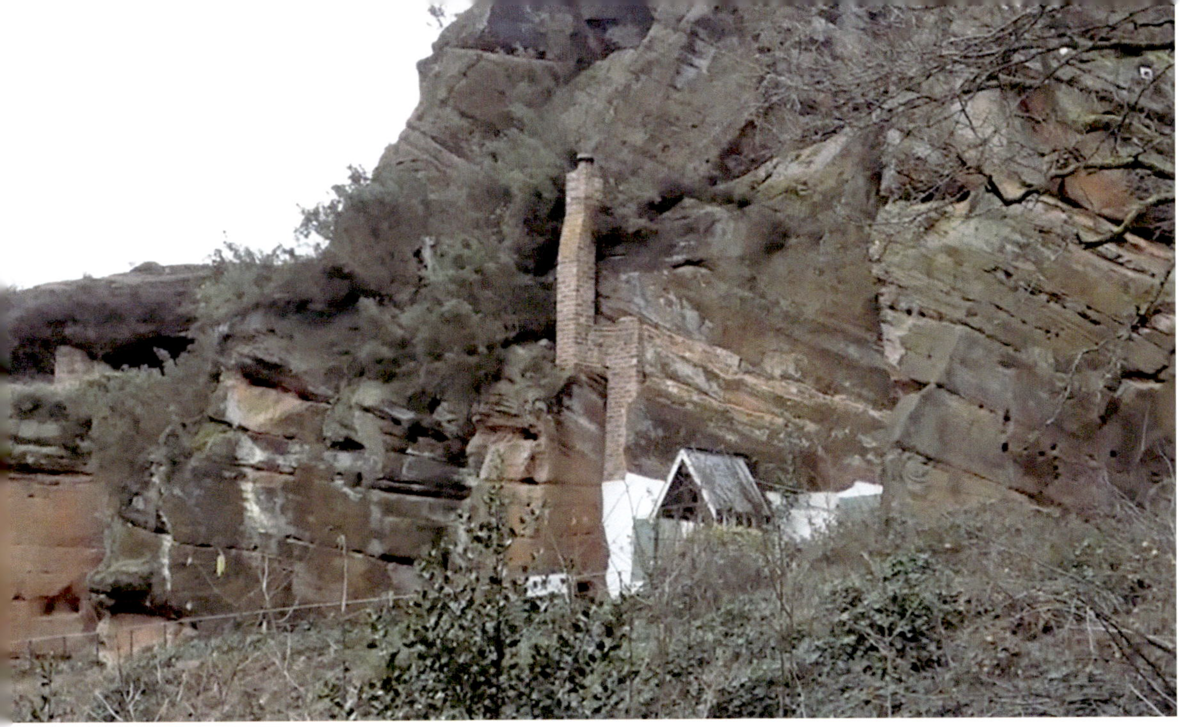

Above: Kinver's famous rock houses.

Below: Kinver Edge rock houses.

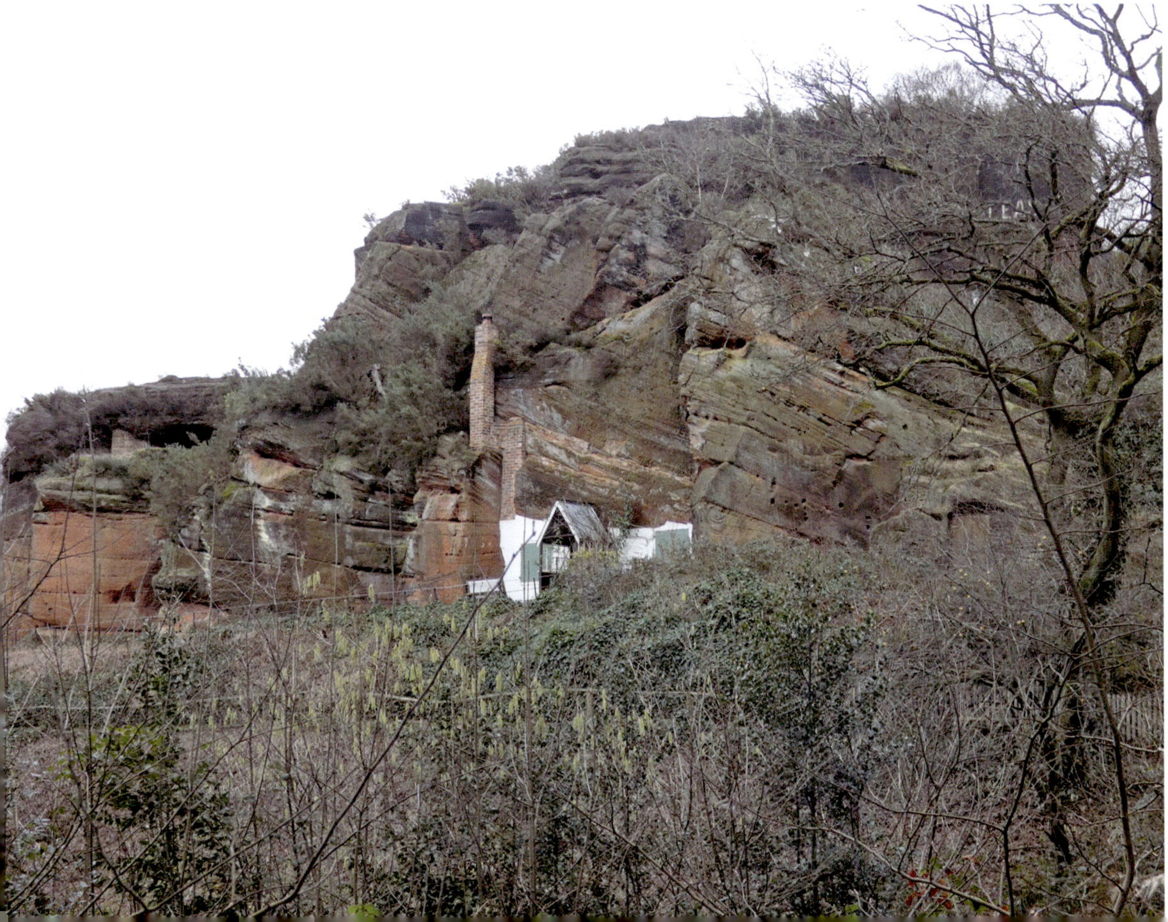

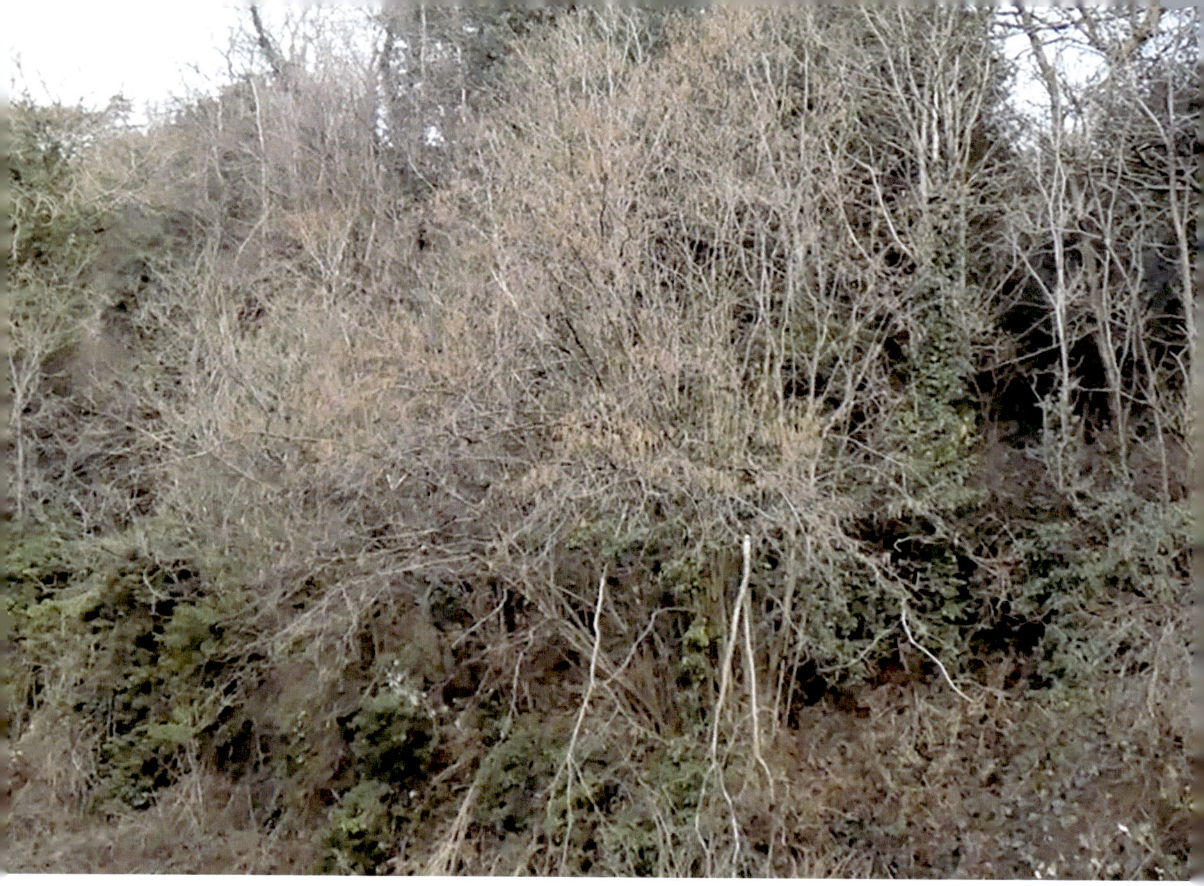

The name of Gibraltar has nothing to do with our interest. The cave houses, which are still in situ, are hidden by the vegetation today.

Giving an idea of the numbers of people living here over the years are the number of burials of those listed for those living in the rock houses of Kinver. Some 150 burials are listed during a seventy-year period in the nineteenth century. If we take those seventy years as representing a lifetime, then it is a reasonable assumption that about the same number would have been living here permanently. We can only wonder what those residents would have thought when, after the opening of the Kinver Light Railway in 1901, Edwardian tourists from other parts of the Midlands, and particularly Birmingham, began using this scenic location for recreation. Remember, this era saw postcards produced en masse, with images of everyday scenes at least as common as those scenic views still seen in later years.

Some entrepreneurial residents clearly did not disapprove of these visitors. Indeed, they took full advantage as there is written evidence of tearooms, such as the Rock House Café which served refreshments. Indeed, the café continued to function until 1967 – several years after all other residents had been rehoused.

3

LOWER PENN AND WOMBOURNE

If anywhere in the Black Country can be said to epitomise the region, especially when it reflects what might be found underground, it would be difficult to find anywhere better than Wombourne and, to the north, Lower Penn. This may only be a small part of the region, but it boasts both canals and railways. Yet neither of these means of travel come through here via a tunnel; both negotiated the region either by the locks, in the case of the canal, or by taking a line where the gradients were at their shallowest, as in the line of the former railway.

Hence, this region will be examined for that buried beneath the ground to supply the region with electricity, gas, water, and oil. It is not only the supplies to individual premises which we are looking at here, but also the main supply feeding the region. Taking these in order, the electricity supply comes to the substations along the overhead cables supported by pylons. No overhead supply for gas supplies, of course, and here there are no less than three different pipelines to view. First the local supply, which follow the lines of the roads. Records show the pressure in this line to be very low: no more than 0.5 psi, and often half that figure.

One up from those lines are the pipes feeding the Regional Grid. With demand for gas fluctuating greatly, the pressure in these pipes can vary from as little as 2 psi to as much as 30 psi. One of these pipes comes through Lower Penn from a governor near Billy Buns Lane to another governor at Spring Hill. In Wombourne, a similar line runs between governors on the Bridgnorth Road at the South Staffordshire Railway Walk and follows that road east to a second governor near where it crosses the Wom Brook.

There is also the pipe of the Supergrid, a pipeline running from the Black Country to the east between Lower Penn and Wombourne, and heading off to Shrewsbury to the west under a pressure of anything from 100 psi to 250 psi, depending upon demand. Running along a line to the west of the region, mirroring the line of the Staffordshire and Worcestershire Canal quite closely, is the Natural Gas Grid's pipeline. This is the under the greatest pressure of them all at 600 psi and, to put that into perspective, is the equivalent of being 1,352 feet below the surface of the sea – enough to submerge the Eiffel Tower and still have 250 feet to spare.

On to water, where the main feeding Lower Penn is a sizable 18 inches in diameter and runs between Wolverhampton to the east and Trescott to the west, with the Dimmingsdale Pumping Station helping it on its way. At Wombourne the Bratch Pumping Station takes water to and from Goldthorpe Mill and Bilston through a 16-inch-diameter main. This pumping station, a delightful piece of architecture, coupled with the nearby Bratch Locks, make for the perfect backdrops to walkers around this area.

Perhaps the most surprising pipeline under Wombourne is that carrying oil from Milford Haven. Almost directly west of the junction of Ebstree Road and Trysull Holloway is where the oil splits into two. One heads north to Manchester, while the other turns just south of east and crosses the Stourbridge Road near where the Lyd Brook and Wom Brook meet before heading off to serve Sedgley, Birmingham, and Nottingham.

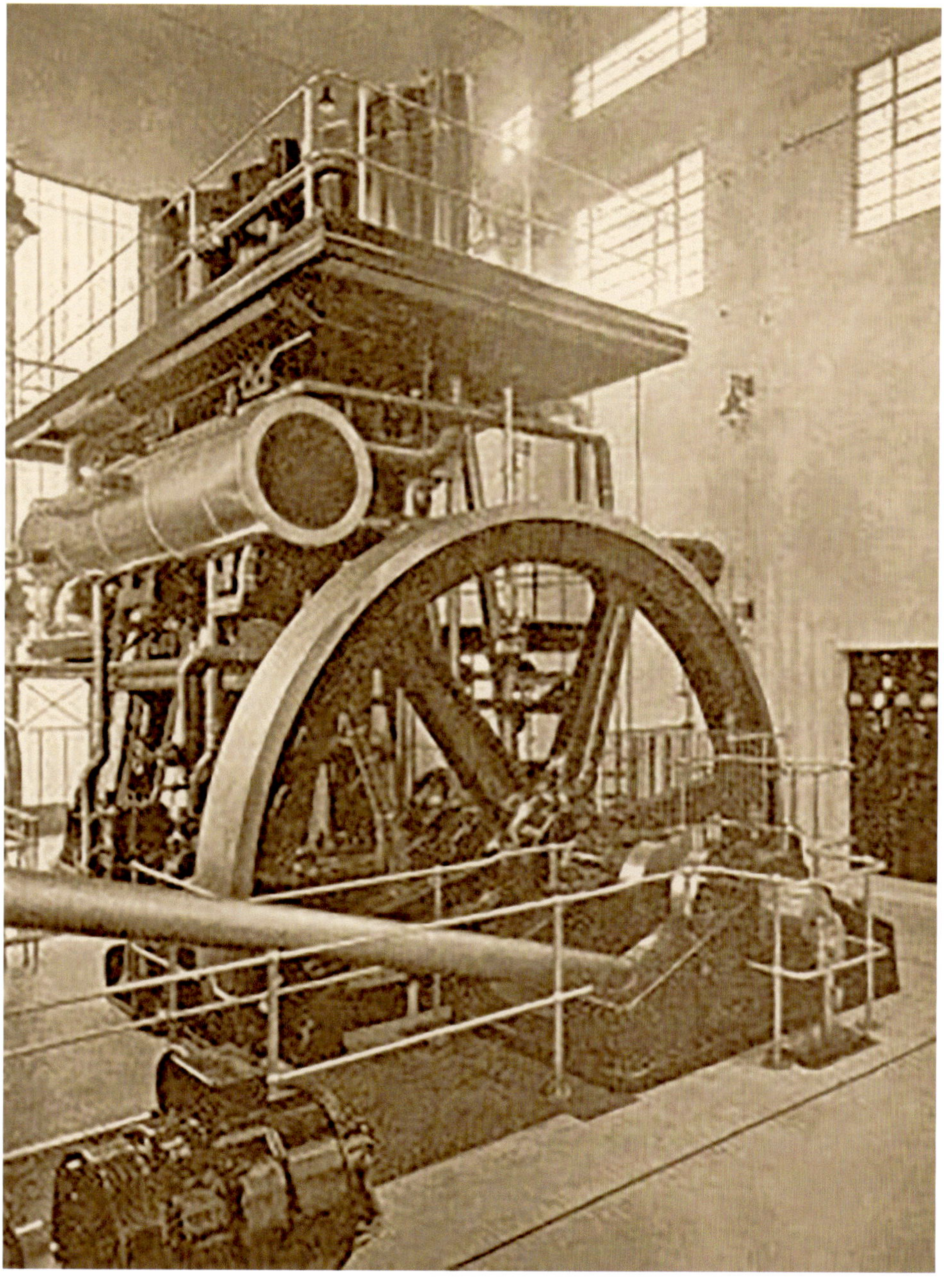

Dimmingsdale Pumping Station. (Courtesy of historywebsite.co.uk)

4

NETHERTON TUNNEL

Netherton Tunnel is not just a story of a tunnel, it is the tale of an entire length of canal. Our story starts in 1855 with the ceremonial cutting of the first sod by William Ward, 1st Earl of Dudley. Three years later, having spent £302,000 instead of the £238,000 budgeted, the new canal opened on 20 August. Built to relieve the bottleneck of the adjacent Dudley Canal which, as we shall see in the following chapter, is very much narrower and less easily navigated.

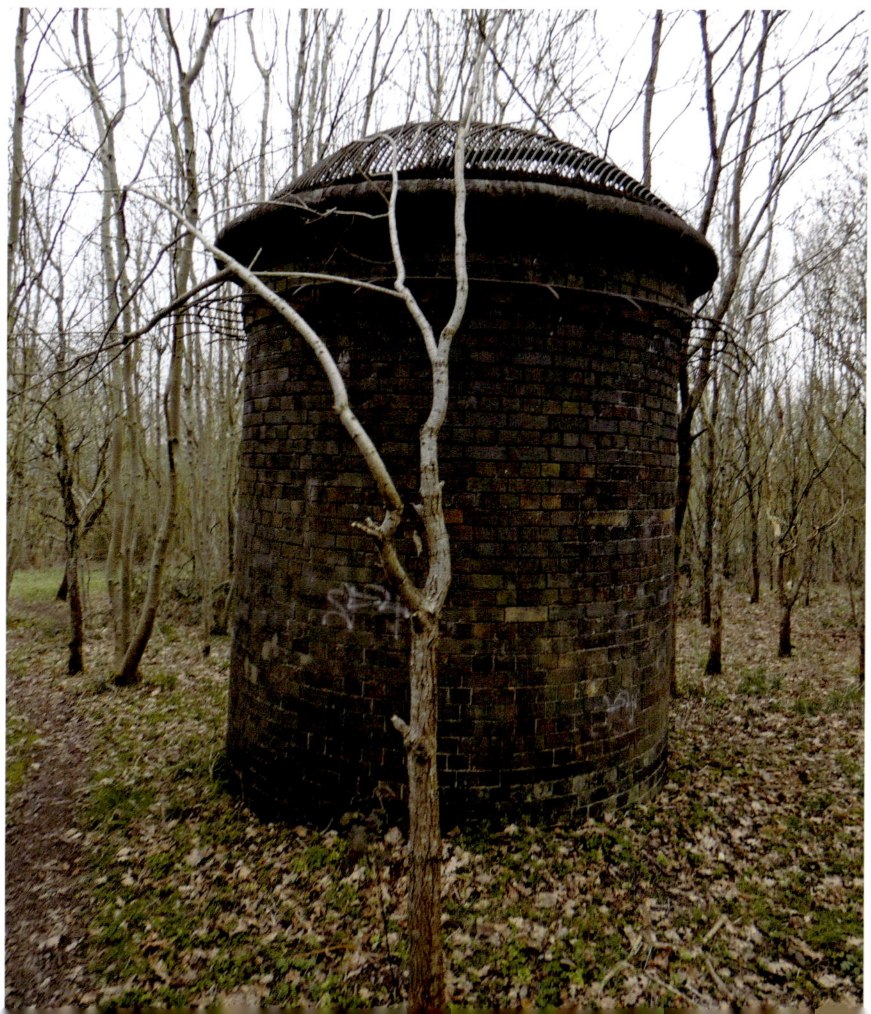

Netherton Tunnel ventilation shaft.

Netherton Tunnel was built 27 feet wide, with towpaths on either side, allowing passage of boats in both directions. This made it the widest canal tunnel in Britain at the time it opened. It was 6 inches wider than that at Strood, albeit Netherton only had a water course 17 feet wide as against 21 feet and 6 inches for Strood. Brick-lined, it was originally lit by gas and later electricity, although today the only illumination is from boats passing through. While the gas-lit tunnel came from a small pipeline, the subsequent electric lighting was powered by a turbine located at the Tividale Aqueduct. Today the pipe can still be seen leading to a brick annexe and driving the water turbine powering the tunnel's ventilation.

There are sixteen ventilation shafts, an indication of the tunnel's length, known as 'pepper pots' by the locals owing to their shape. It is correctly known as the Netherton Tunnel Branch Canal as most of its length is tunnel – while the canal is only 2.4 miles in length, more than 70 per cent of that length is tunnel. By including towpaths on both sides, horse-drawn boats were able to be pulled through, while the air vents mean boats powered by internal-combustion engines are allowed to come through today.

Running from Warrens Hall Park to Dudley Road West (the canal covering the route from Dudley Port to Tividale), the ground here is difficult to tunnel through, as discovered with the building of the adjacent Dudley Canal. An overspend of £64,000 due to these same difficulties, and those problems continue to reveal themselves. In 1983, some 80 yards of brickwork had to be replaced with concrete as the bricks had moved to such an extent it would soon prove a problem to navigation, this despite a maximum clearance of 16 feet. British Waterways kept the tunnel closed to traffic from 1980 to 1984. In 2011, cracks were discovered in the tunnel lining and traffic limited for two years until repairs, started in 2013, were completed.

A coal-laden canal barge stuck in an ice-bound canal. The boatman appears to be trying to free the boat. The exact date and location are unknown. (Ref: p/2105, courtesy of the T. W. King collection held at Dudley Archives & Local History Service)

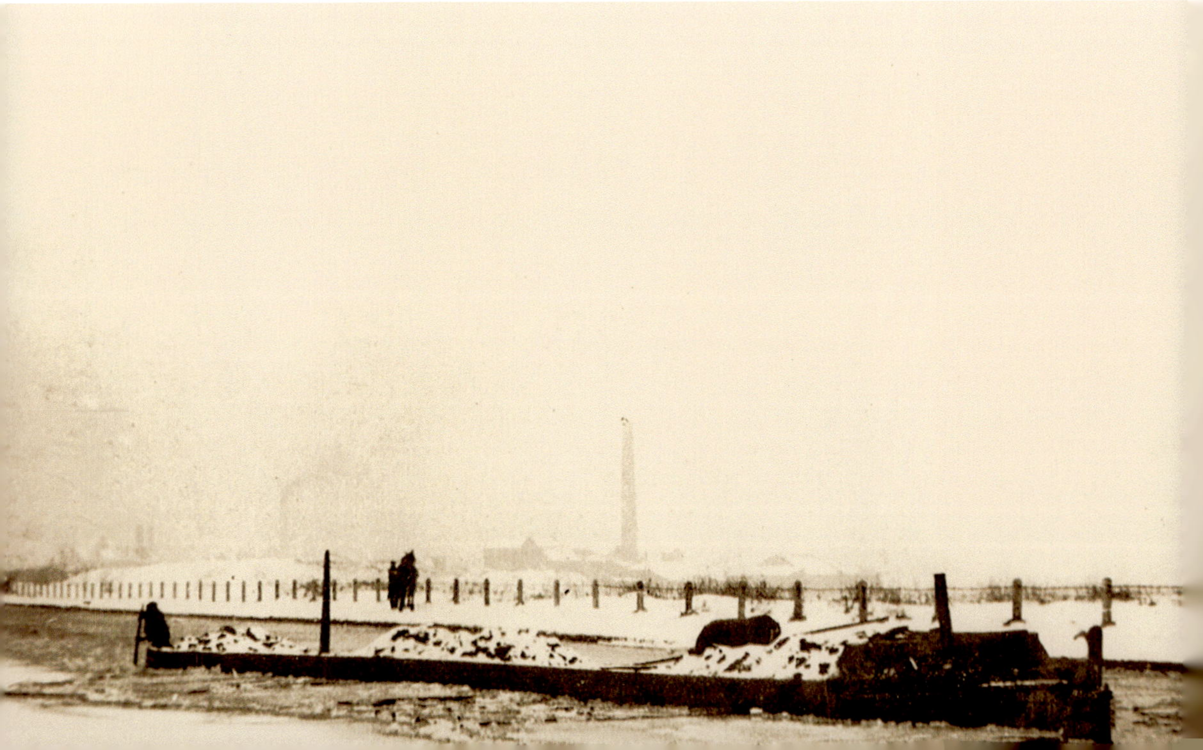

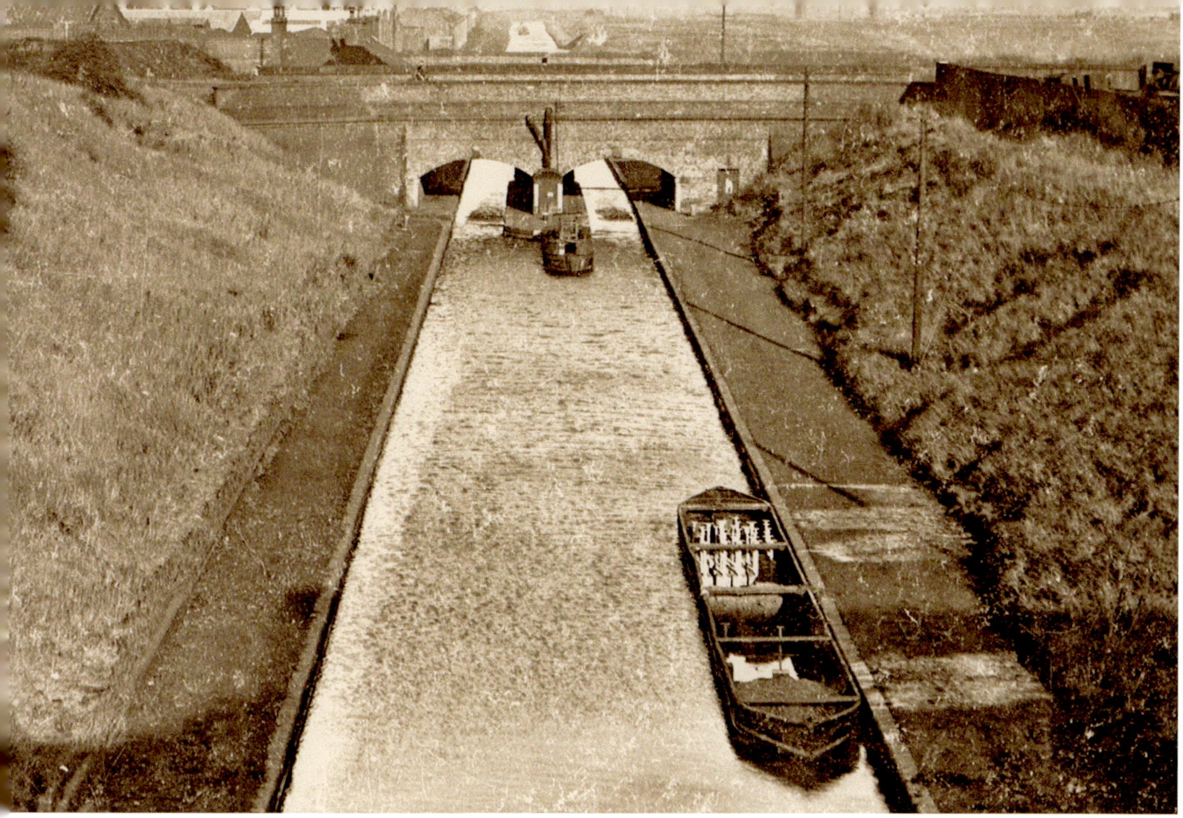

Above: A view, taken from a height, of Groveland Bridge (often referred to as Tividale Aquaduct), which carries the Birmingham Canal Navigations' (BCN) Wolverhampton Level Old Main Line Canal over the BCN Netherton Tunnel Branch. This view emphasises the straightness of the canal. The small building in between the two arches was used to house a generator to provide electricity for lighting Netherton Tunnel. It was powered by water from the canal above. The canal barge in the foreground appears to be carrying coal. It is unknown what the white objects in the barge are, although it is suggested that they provided a frame for holding a cargo of spelter (zinc). (Ref: p/2136, courtesy of the T. W. King collection held at Dudley Archives & Local History Service)

Below: The south portal of Netherton Canal Tunnel.

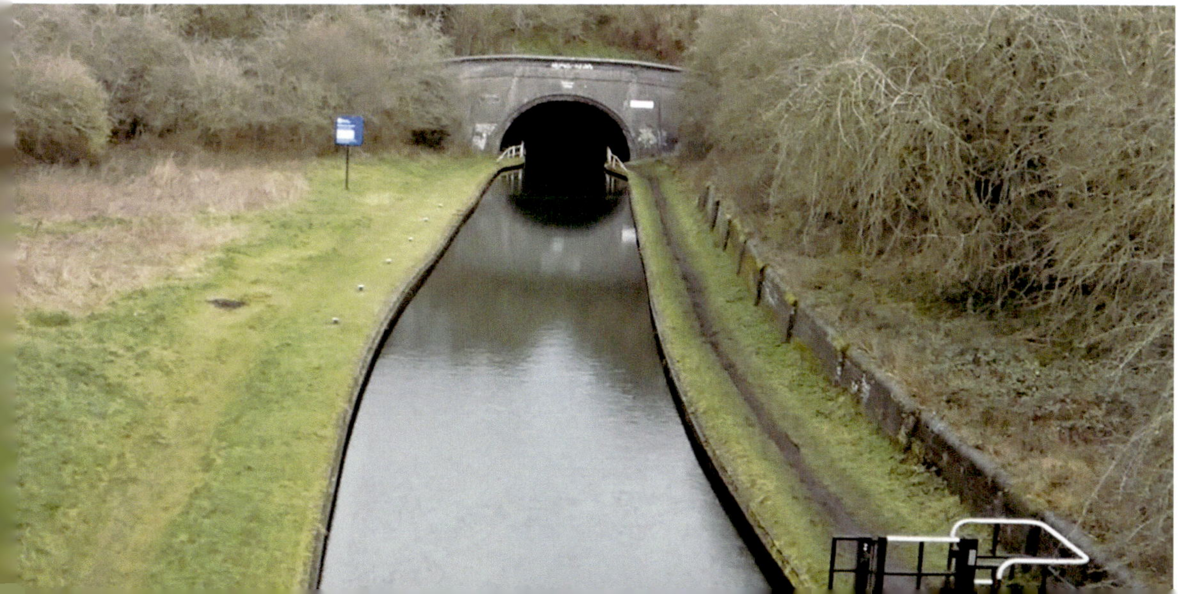

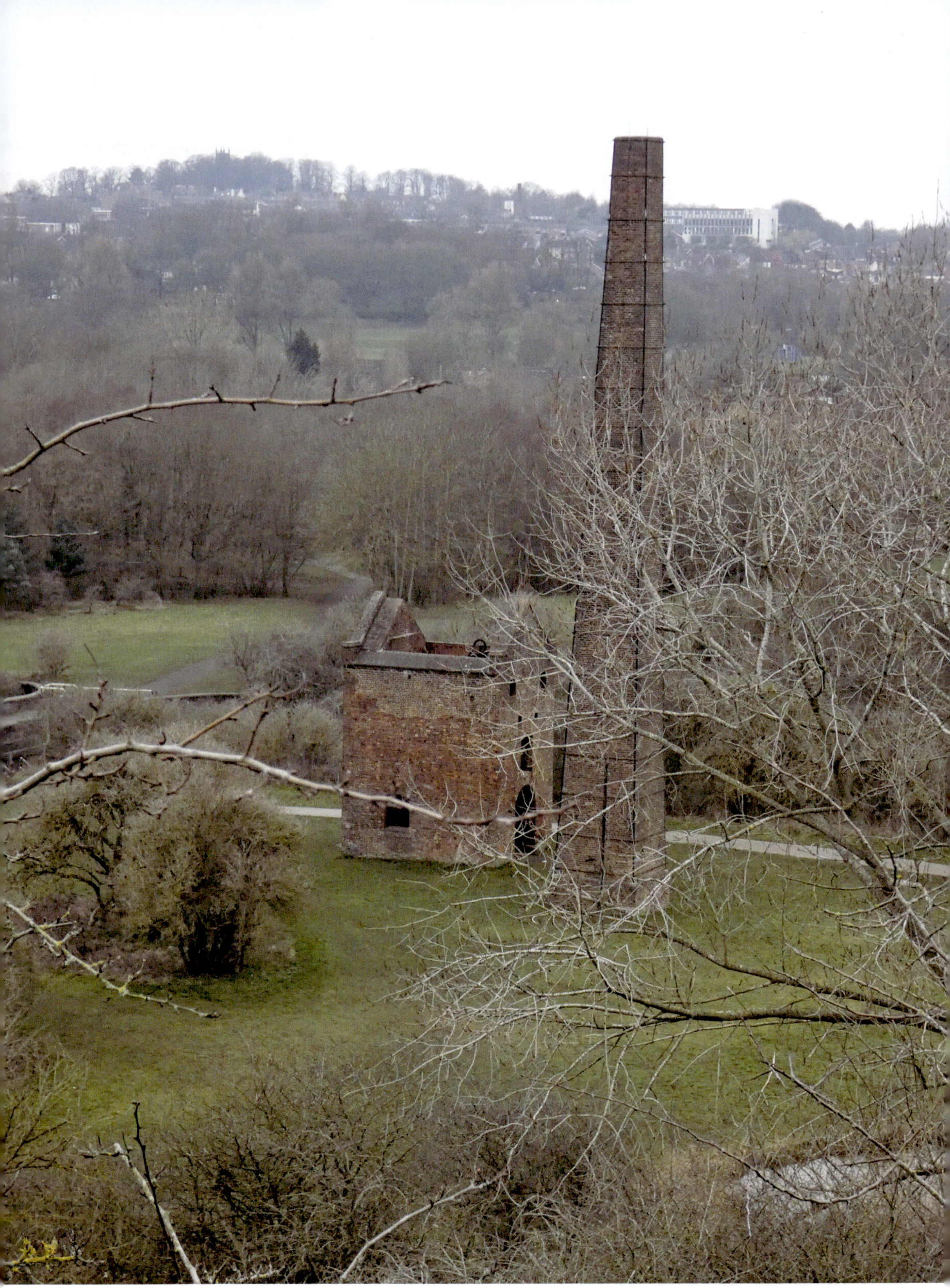

Cobb's Engine House at Warrens Hall Nature Reserve.

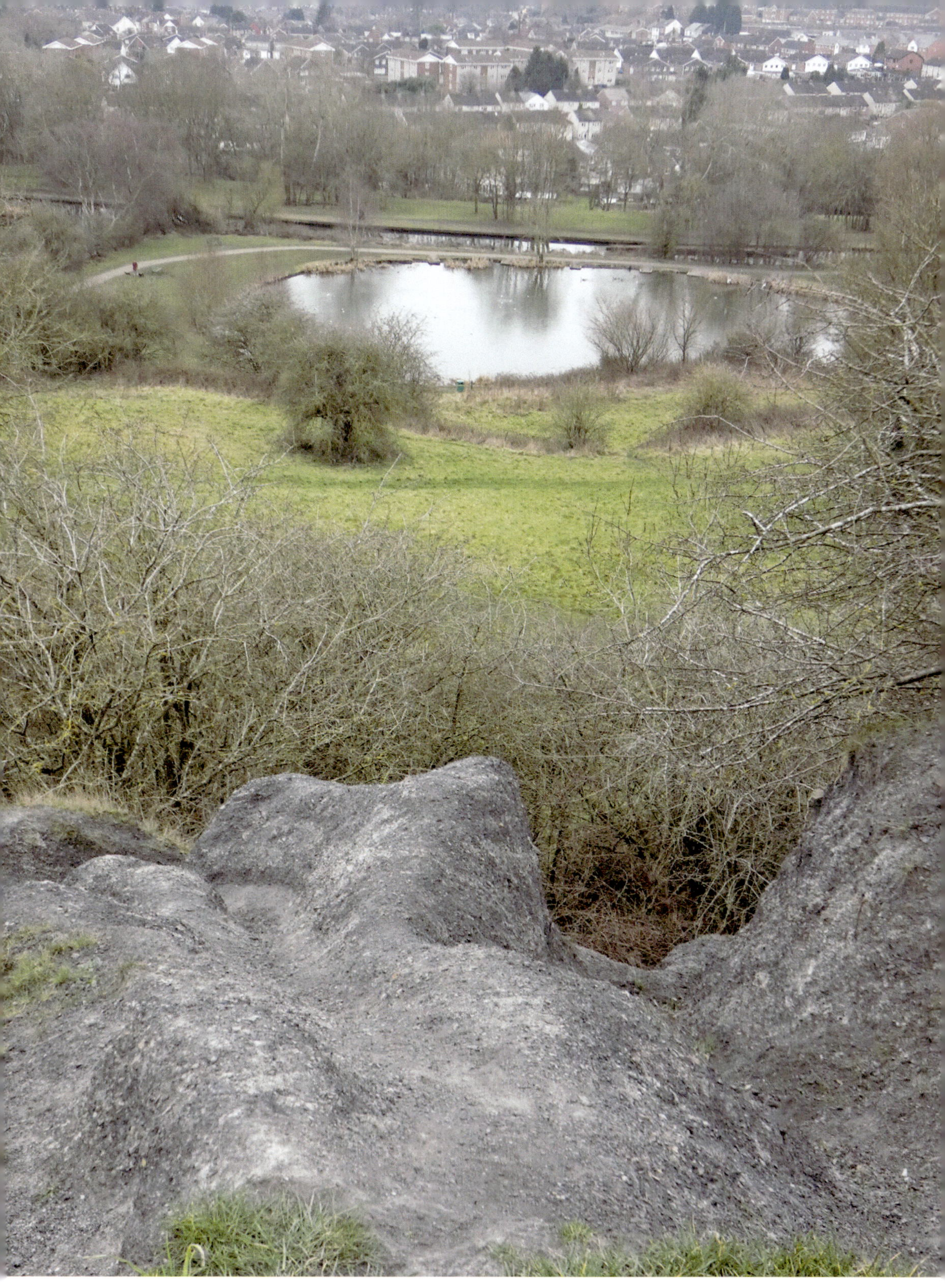

Another view of Warrens Hall Nature Reserve.

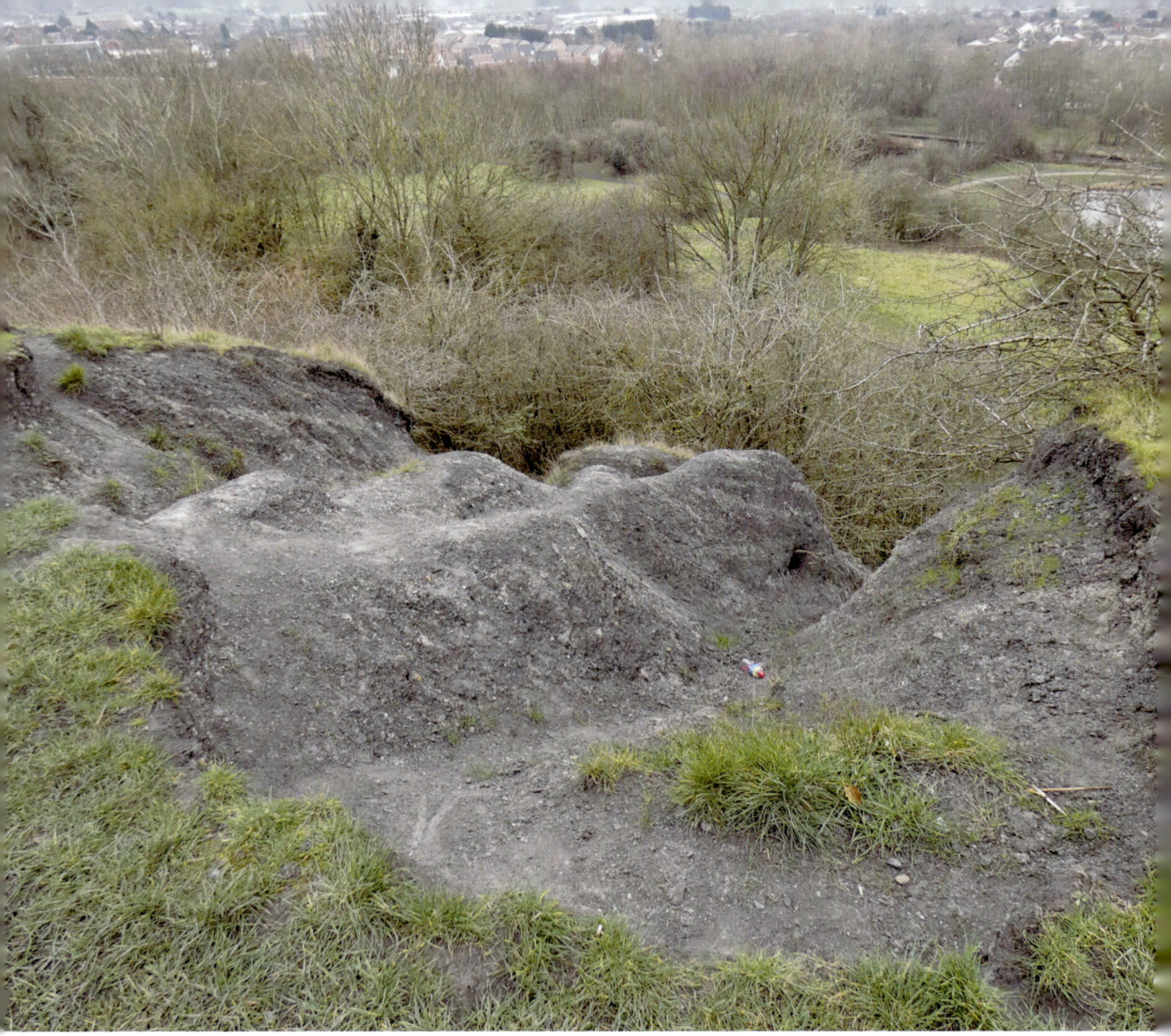

A final look at the reserve shows the spoil heap is still in situ.

Yet perhaps the most unexpected problem came in 2002 when slippage of the tunnel roof occurred because of an earthquake measuring 4.7 on the Richter scale. While the effects were felt across England and Wales on 22 September, that the epicentre was nearby meant it was recorded as the Dudley Earthquake.

What is most fascinating about this tunnel and canal is the date of construction, for the 1850s is a decade when railways are the principal means of travel and lines are still expanding at a rapid rate. In fact, Netherton Tunnel was the last canal tunnel built in the age of canals, albeit those days already seen as numbered. Furthermore, its construction uses techniques not employed for anything other than railway tunnels prior to this. Indeed, this so obviously a railway construction that it has been referred to on numerous occasions through the years as a 'flooded railway tunnel'.

5

DUDLEY TUNNEL

As mentioned in the previous chapter, Dudley Tunnel was created earlier than Netherton Tunnel. It was completed on 14 June 1779 and connected the canals serving the limestone workings owned by Lord Dudley and Ward and Thomas Talbot Foley to the Birmingham Canal. As noted for the construction of the Netherton Canal, this involved tunnelling through ground that did not lend itself well to such engineering. Furthermore, engineers were having to do so in what is a very long tunnel, which explains why this cutting had originally been planned without a tunnel.

Correctly, this canal was an extension of an earlier branch canal, known as the Lord Dudley & Ward's Branch Canal. Completed and working on 1 June 1778, this is a private cut into the Tipton colliery, later extended into Castle Mill. Originally the plan had been to build five locks to raise this level to Park Head, then connecting via a tunnel to the Dudley Canal. Graciously, Lord Dudley consented to sell on the terms to the Birmingham

The works (possibly the ironworks) of Noah Hingley & Sons Ltd on the Dudley No. 2 Canal at Netherton. Coal-laden barges can be seen on the canal. The bridge over the canal was actually two private bridges. Note the extensive use of the canal by the company. (Ref: p2196, courtesy of Dudley Archives and Local History Service)

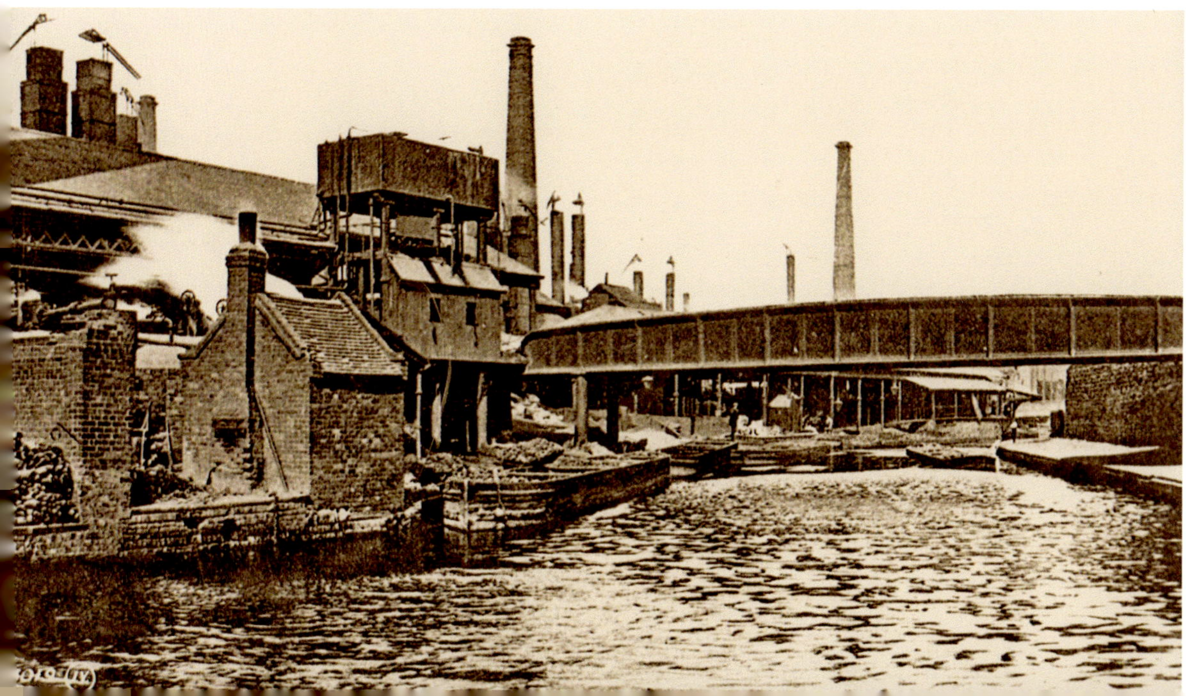

company, who would then be able to collect tolls. But this never materialised, for the purchaser argued they should not have to buy that stretch of canal as Lord Dudley already earned favourable tolls from his earlier canal. Astonishingly, this was not only agreed but the new owners also managed to increase tolls significantly.

These combined canals and tunnels are best viewed when entering from the Tipton end, where the railway passes overhead. The first 200 yards passes old workings, including those of the Tipton Colliery to the right and former limestone mine on the left. After passing through the galleries, it emerges into the Castle Mill Basin; here we will look to the tunnel to the right first. This runs for 1,227 yards and includes a loading basin and passing bay around the mid-point, before emerging at Wren's Nest Basin where, in 1840, 240 steps on a spiral staircase led down from the surface.

Returning to the Castle Mill Basin to take the left option at the fork, we very soon come to another side tunnel on the left. This once led to the Castle Mill Quarries, with a terminal loading basin. This has long been unreachable owing to a roof fall a short way into this side tunnel. What we do know is there was another tunnel off this stretch shortly after where the roof has collapsed. Leading to the quarry shaft and gallery, a sunken boat once lay even before the collapse and, presumably, still lies complete with clues as to its history and its demise. Carrying on along the original line, these 2,942 yards is not all man-made. Shortly before the end we find an air shaft and, almost immediately after, a natural cavern. It is but another short stretch until approaching the exit, which is clearly from a different era, being rebuilt in 1884.

Dudley Canal Tunnel illuminated by the Dudley Canal boat tour.

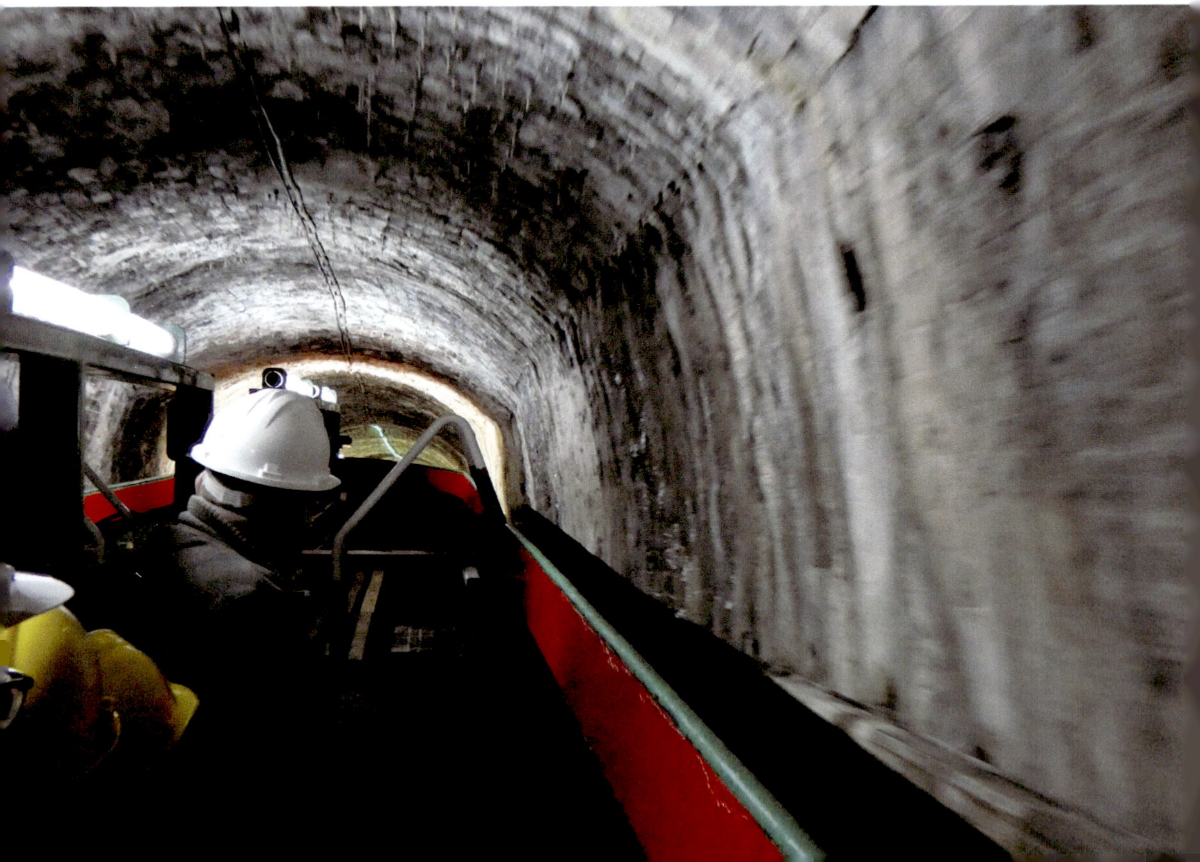

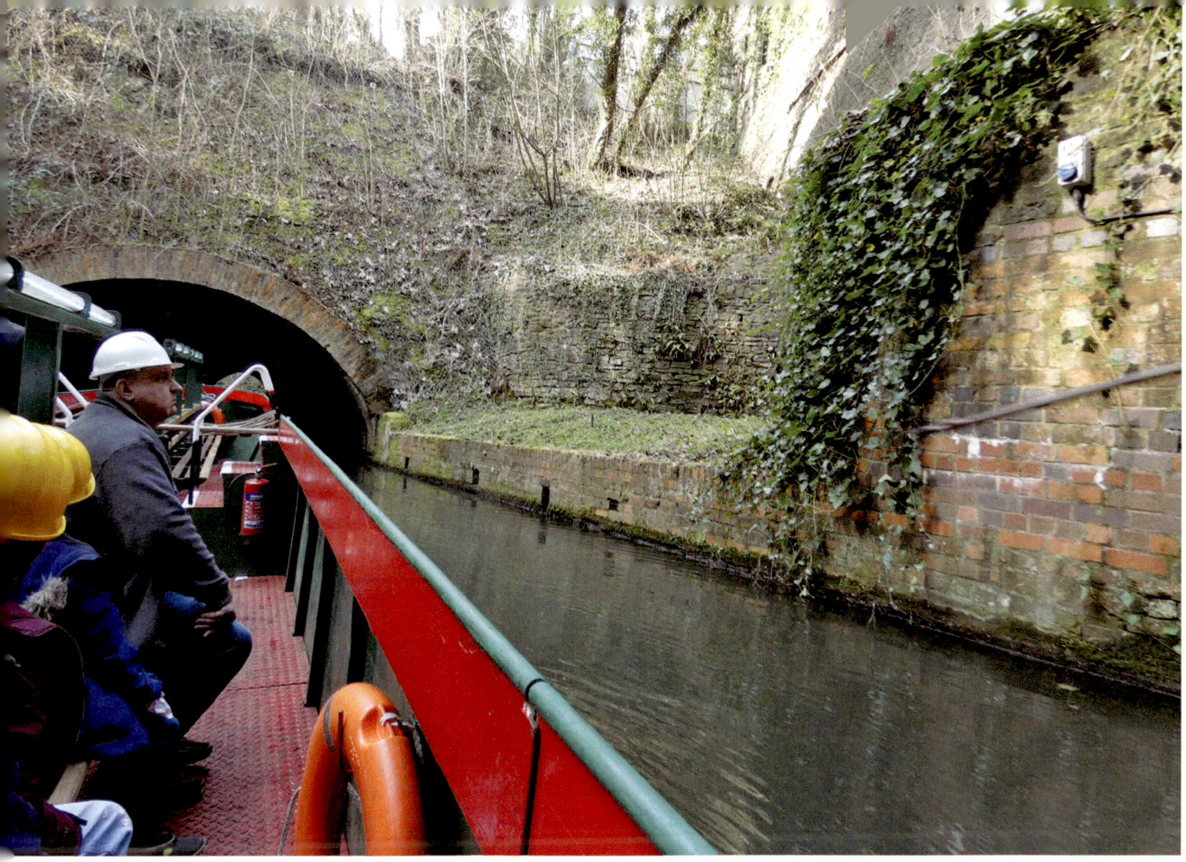

Above: Basin on the Dudley Canal formed by mining the limestone.

Below: Disused tunnel on the Dudley Canal.

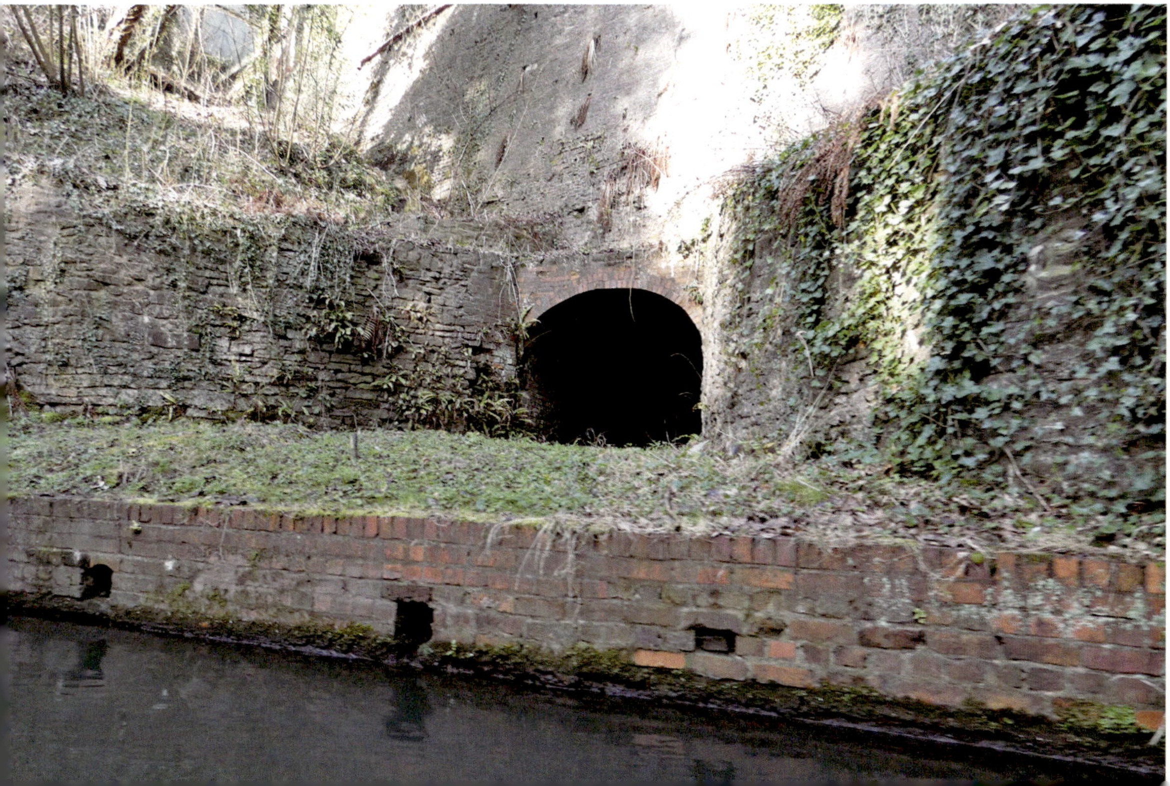

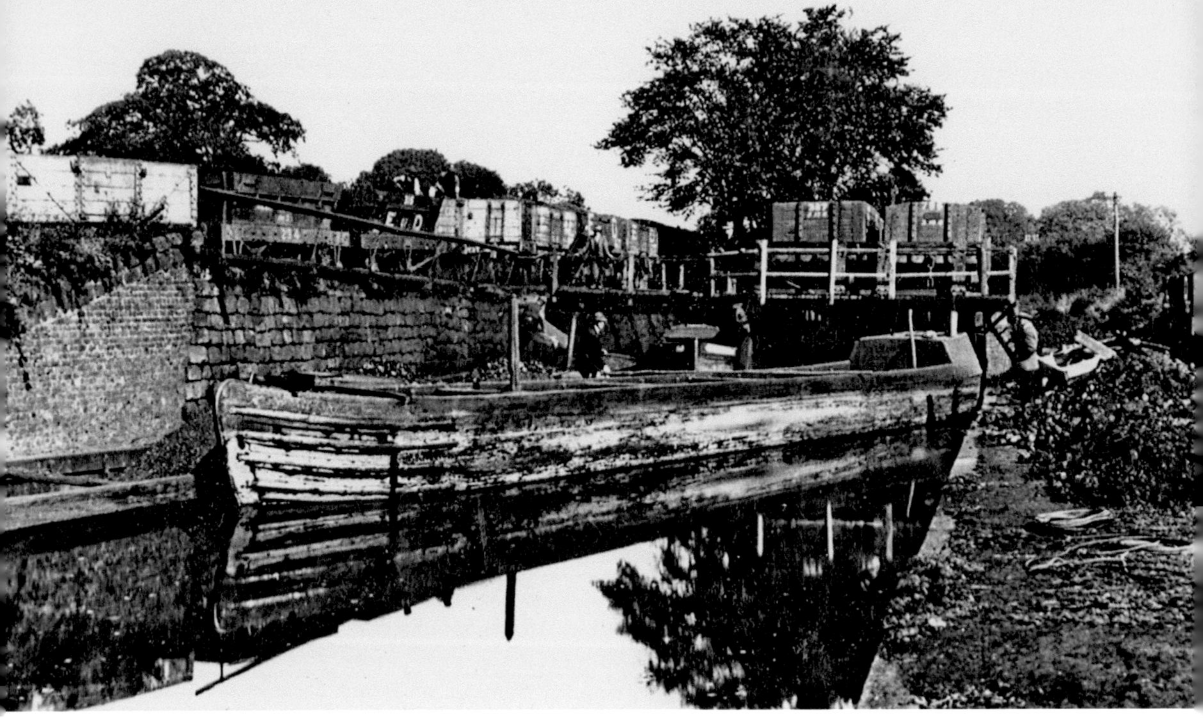

Above: Coal from one of the Earl of Dudley's coal mines (note the 'E of D' on four of the coal trucks) either being loaded or unloaded onto a coal barge on what is possibly Ashwood Basin. The barge looks like it is being manoeuvred into position for the coal, judging by the fact that it is at an angle across the canal. (Ref: p/1851, courtesy of Dudley Archives and Local History Service)

Below: The roof of Dudley Canal Tunnel still shows the marks made from the excavator's tools.

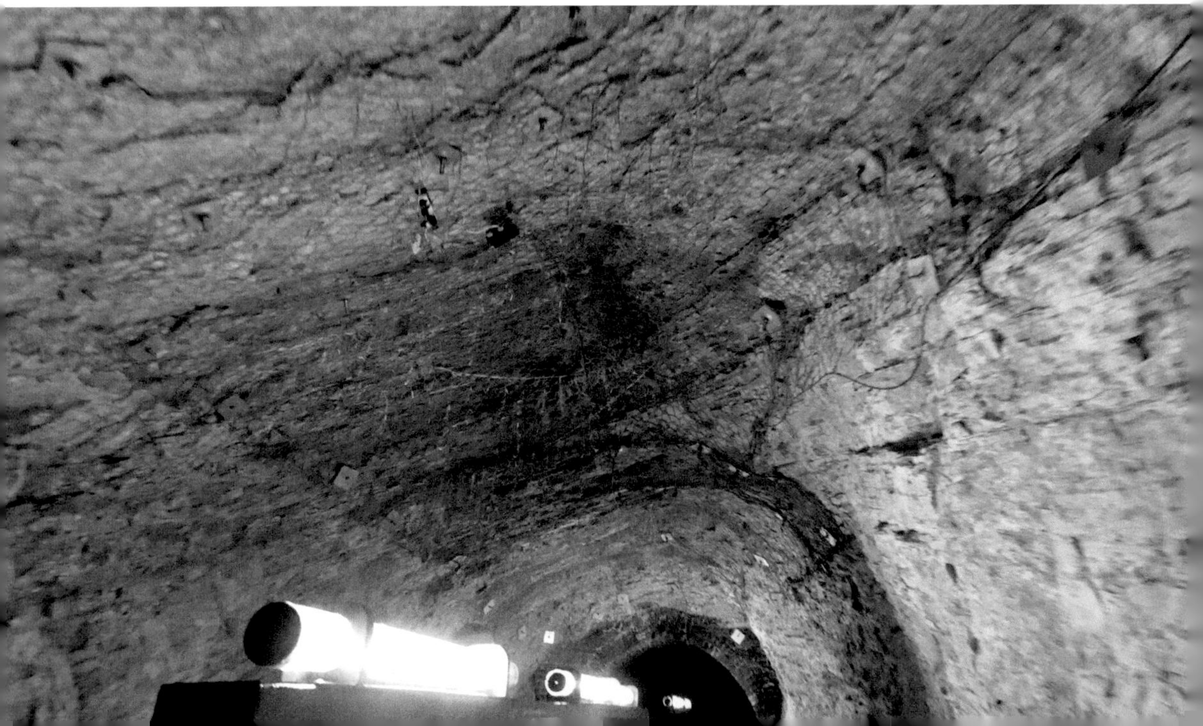

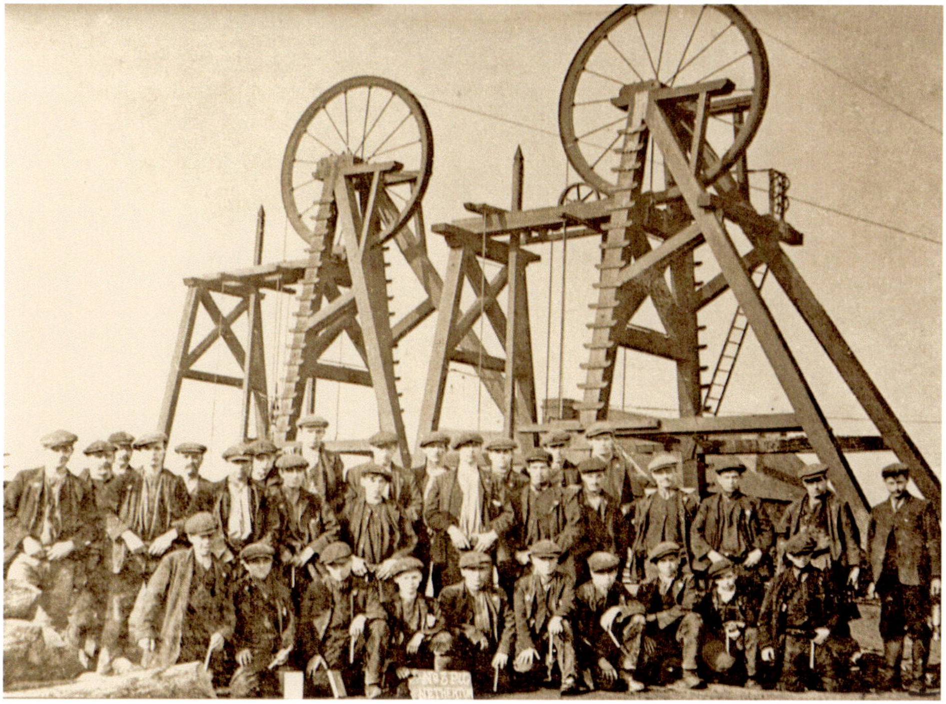

Coal miners and mining equipment *c.* 1900. (Ref: p/3019, courtesy of Dudley Archives and Local History Service)

Unlike the Netherton Tunnel which followed, the Dudley Tunnel does not boast even a single towpath, nor will it permit the passage of boats in opposing directions over most of its length. By only allowing lines of boats to pass through in one direction at a time, this led to a bottleneck where boats could easily wait more than eight hours to enter the tunnel and sometimes be stranded here for days. Remember, with no towpath the horse could not provide motive power and leggers would propel the boat through the narrow tunnel by lying on their backs on a plank of wood placed across the boat and walk the walls through, moving sideways like a crab.

This slow, laborious, and exhausting process required two leggers to walk the boat through 3,172 yards of tunnel – the second longest in the country today. Although this seemingly did not deter many, for the tunnel provided access to a record 41,000 boats in 1853 – over a hundred every day. At that time the project was unpopular with established canal routes. They feared new cuttings would ruin their business and reduce the money taken in tolls. Thus, the owners announced they would reduce the tolls from 2*d* to 1½*d* on the Stourbridge Canal, and from 1½*d* to 1*d* on the main line. Not only did this turn out not to be a sales pitch, but they even introduced the new rates before the canal was anywhere near completed.

Yet just over a century later, in 1959, the tunnel was virtually disused and British Waterways announced plans to close it. Protests ensued, including bringing boats through, but after prolonged negotiations British Waterways closed the tunnel in 1962. Proposed changes to the railway line at the northern portal never materialised, as it was affected by the so-called Beeching cuts, meaning the tunnel mouth remained accessible.

Over the next twenty years various projects were tried, and with limited success, but these did keep the canal and tunnel open, and when the Black Country Museum took on the project at the northern portal, it enabled visitors to experience the tunnel on its own boat. Note this is battery powered, for the poor ventilation and narrow confines mean diesel and petrol-driven engines are not allowed. Alternatively, boats can still be legged through, although this is more a visitor experience than a serious means of propulsion.

In 1979 subsidence about a quarter of a mile from the south entrance had to be attended to, and the tunnel closed while repairs were undertaken. It took ten years for the £730,000 funding to be raised and resulted in a widening of that area. However, this resulted in an enlargement of the tunnel leading to the exit and warning signs had to be erected to tell boats the exit would not allow the passage of the largest modern boats.

In 1984, with visitor numbers increasing, a new circular tunnel loop was planned to give access to the Singing Cavern – named for the whistling the wind created when limestone was mined in the eighteenth century – and Little Tess Cavern. Completed in 1990, inside fifteen years visitor numbers had risen to almost 90,000 annually.

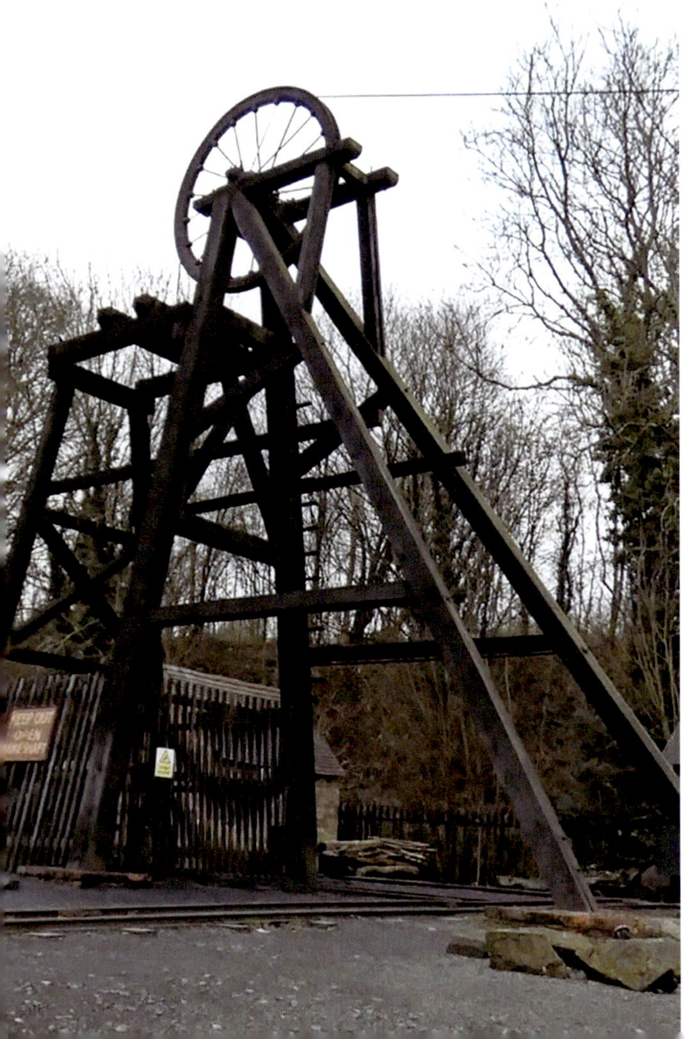

Black Country Museum mine.

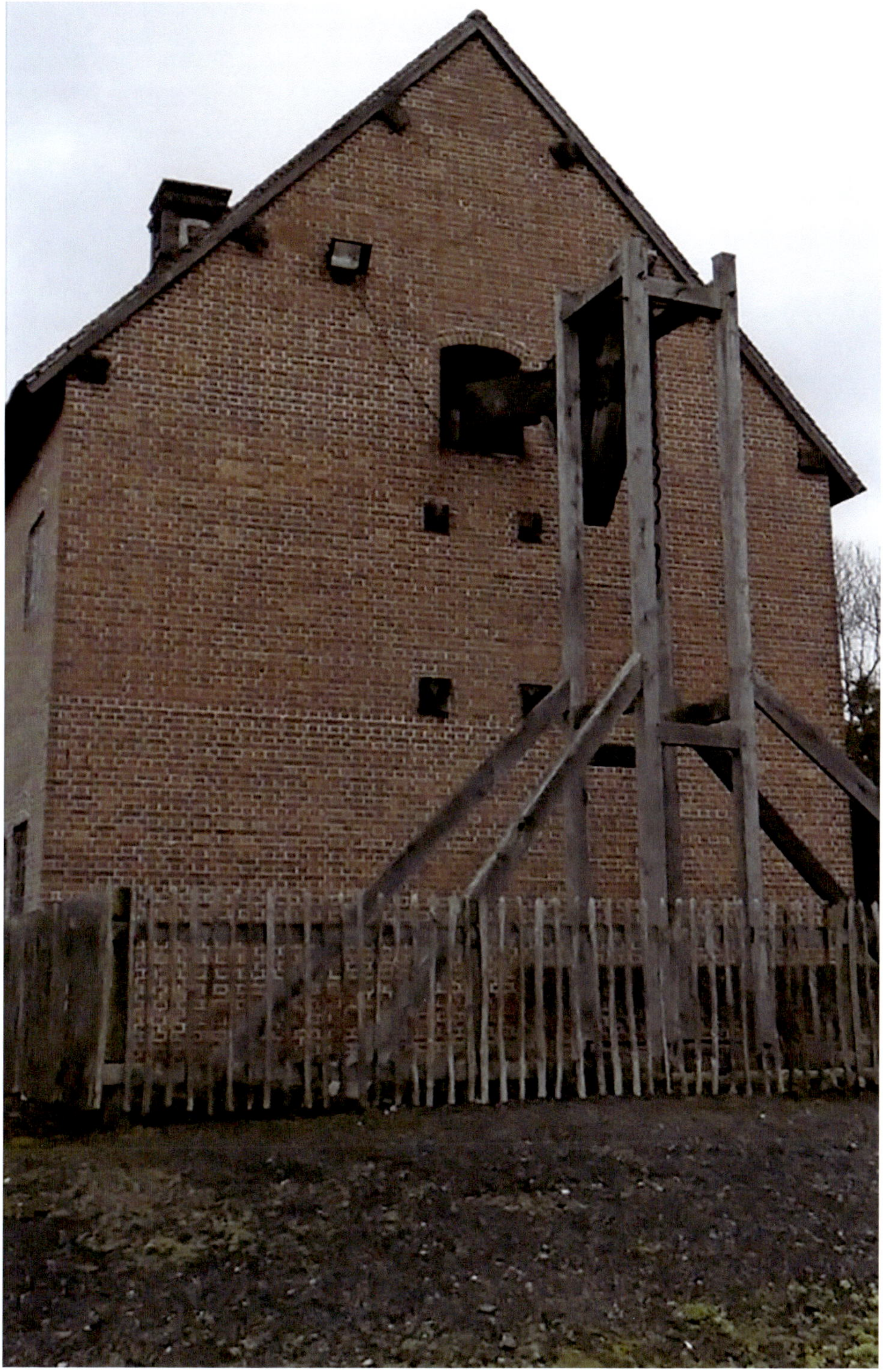

Black Country Museum Newcomen Pumping House.

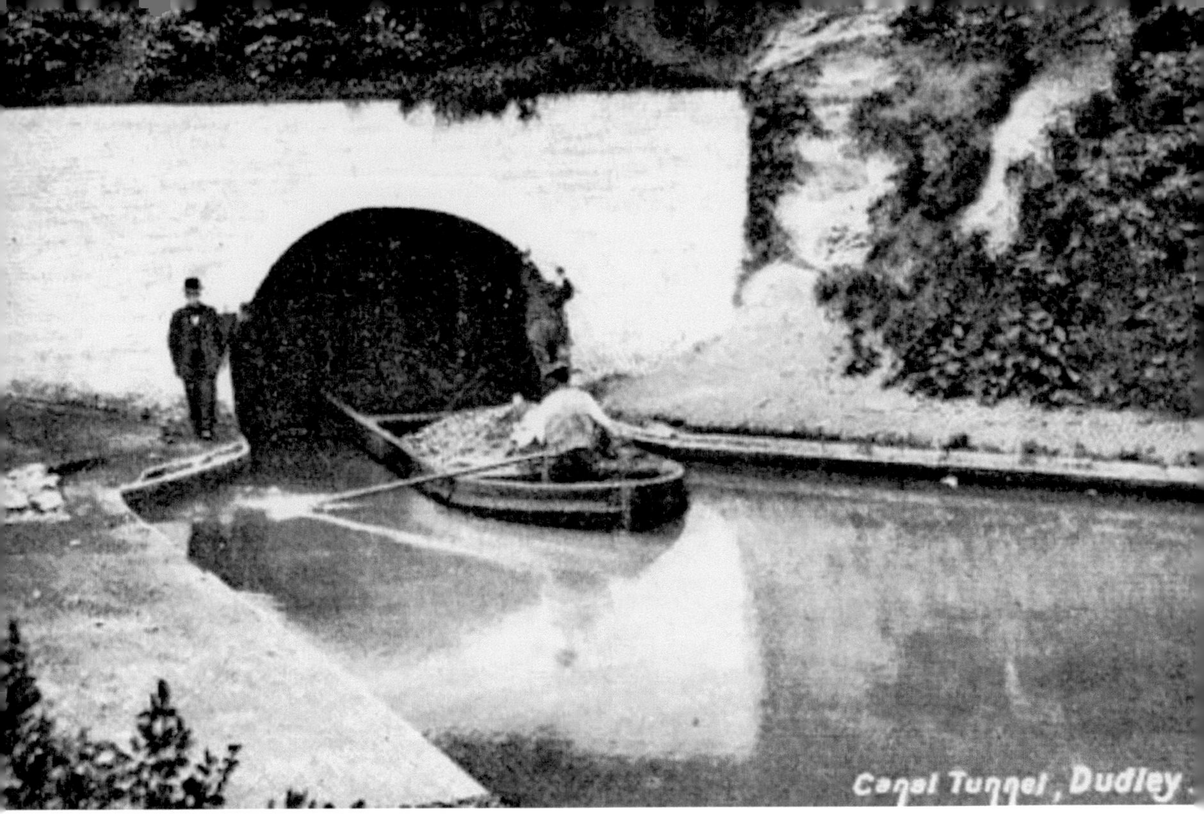

Above: Canal tunnel, Dudley. From a postcard dated to the early 1900s.

Below: East end of Dudley Tunnel, summer 1964. (Robin Webster, CC BY-SA 2.0)

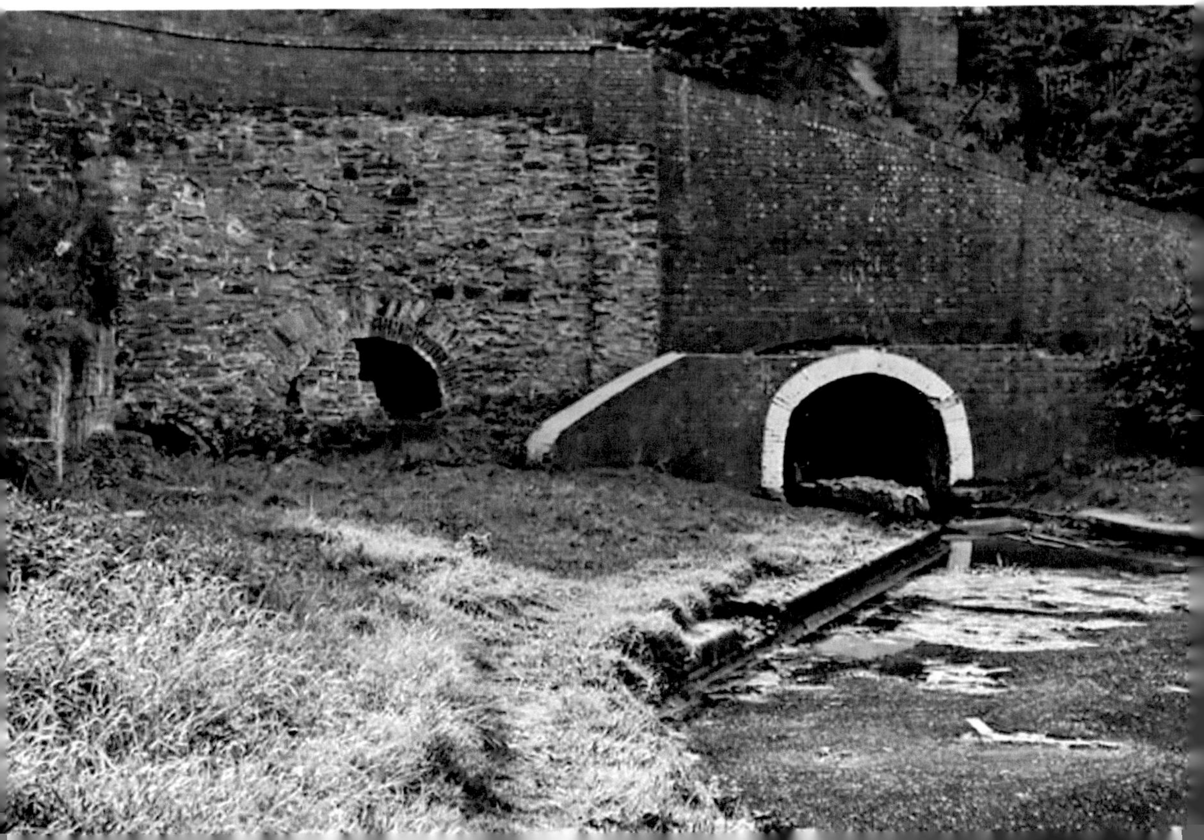

6

LAPAL TUNNEL

If anyone should be engineering a canal tunnel, perhaps being born with the name Underhill will give an applicant a head start. William Underhill designed the Lapal Tunnel, originally known as Lappal, which opened in 1798. At 3,795 yards long, it is among the longest canal tunnels ever constructed in this country – hence the need for no less than thirty ventilation shafts and three steam engines for pumping. Conversely, with a bore of 7 feet 9 inches and a clearance of only 6 feet, it is among the tightest passages to be negotiated by canal boats in the land. Indeed, with a width of 7 feet 9 inches, this is hardly wider than the width of most boats.

Construction of the tunnel proved problematic, for running water through the sand had to be negotiated for approximately three-quarters of the entire length. Three pumps were required to remove the large amount of water present within the rock being tunnelled through. Whilst the removal of water might seem counter intuitive in a project designed to bring water through the hill via a tunnel, it took three engines to remove the underground water trapped in the rocks which, when given an escape route through the tunnel, would have eroded much of the work in a very short time.

While Underhill had been given a house on site and £150 per annum in salary for designing the tunnel, putting that design into practice was the work of engineer Josiah Clowes. Appointed in 1794, he received 3 guineas a day and 4 guineas for every journey made. Such lavish spending on salaries is an indication of how the Industrial Revolution not only changed the lives of most people, who were now employed in factories instead of the nation's farms, but pushed the wages for those with the new technical knowledge as demand for their services accelerated.

At the beginning of 1796, just over a year into the work, Clowes died, and the work fell on Underhill for the next year. A third engineer, Robert Whitworth, came to inspect the work when nearing completion, and a written report by Thomas Brettell spoke of how all the engineers and the workers on the tunnel had initially made mistakes but had learned. Mistakes such as cutting the Halesowen to Netherton section a foot too high to connect with other cuttings. Their work was praised under conditions likened to having 'cleaned the Augean Stables'.

While the narrow width will have made legging the tunnel rather easier, it would also have been rather claustrophobic. The shallow depth also meant boats could be polled through, like the method used to punt boats, but much more strenuous owing to the significant weight of a canal boat even without a cargo. An additional aid to navigating the tunnel came in 1841, in the form of a steam-driven scoop wheel at the Halesowen end. With stop gates at either end, by scooping water from the canal into the trough between the stop gates, it raised the level and provided a head of water.

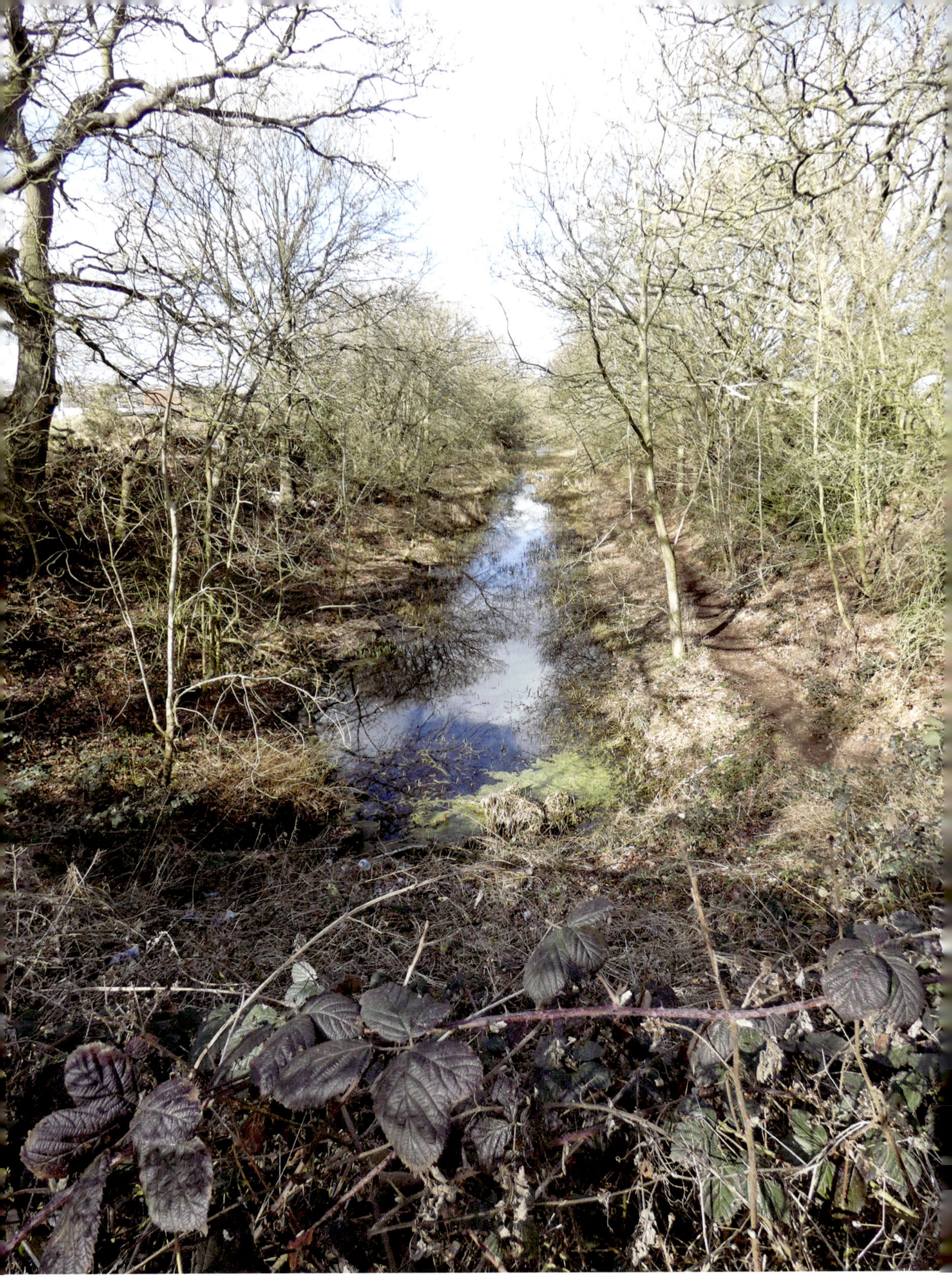

A former branch of the canal once used by Landywood Colliery.

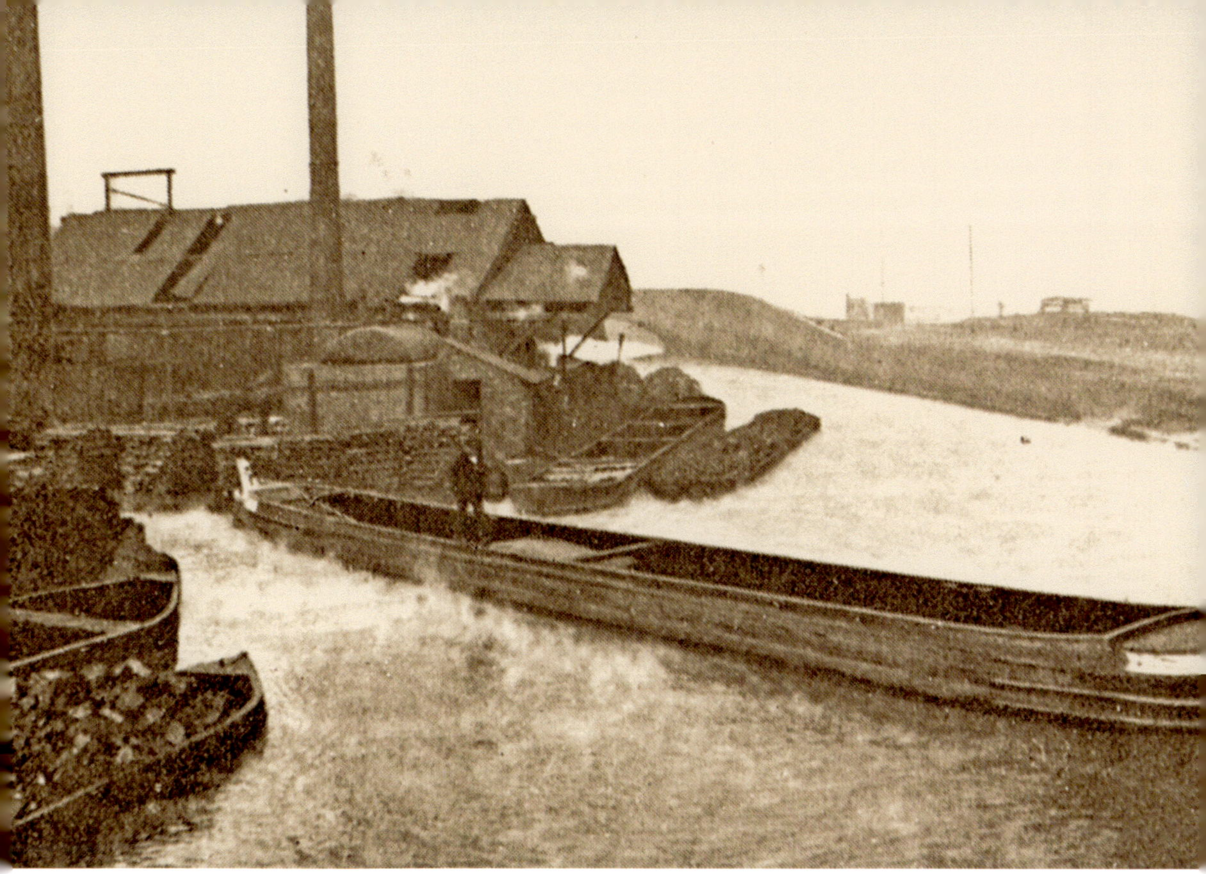

Above: An unladen butty (unpowered) boat on its way out of a basin after discharging its load. The basin is on the lower part of the Wednesbury Oak Loop (just south of the British Waterways depot), part of the old BCN Old Main Line, near Bradley. Laden boats of coal and other unidentified materials (next to the building in crates) can also be clearly seen. The steam coming off the canal would most likely have been the result of the works alongside discharging the water back into the canal after it was initially pumped out for their boilers. The water would have returned to the canal warmer than the surrounding water, causing it to turn into steam. (Ref: p/2175, courtesy of Dudley Archives and Local History Service)

Below: Above the Lapal Tunnel.

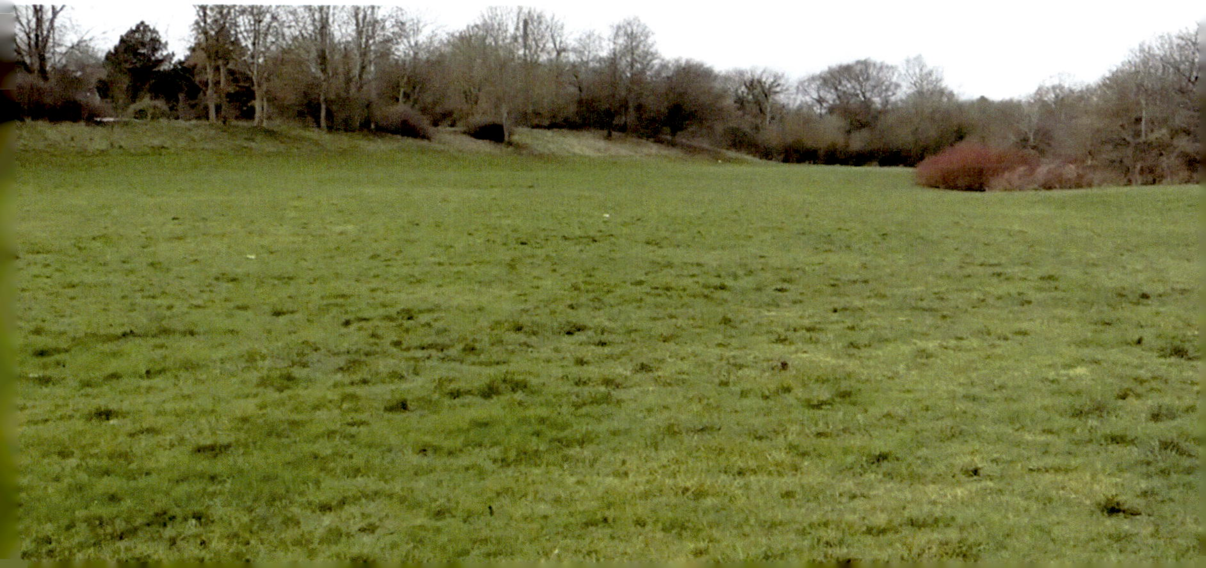

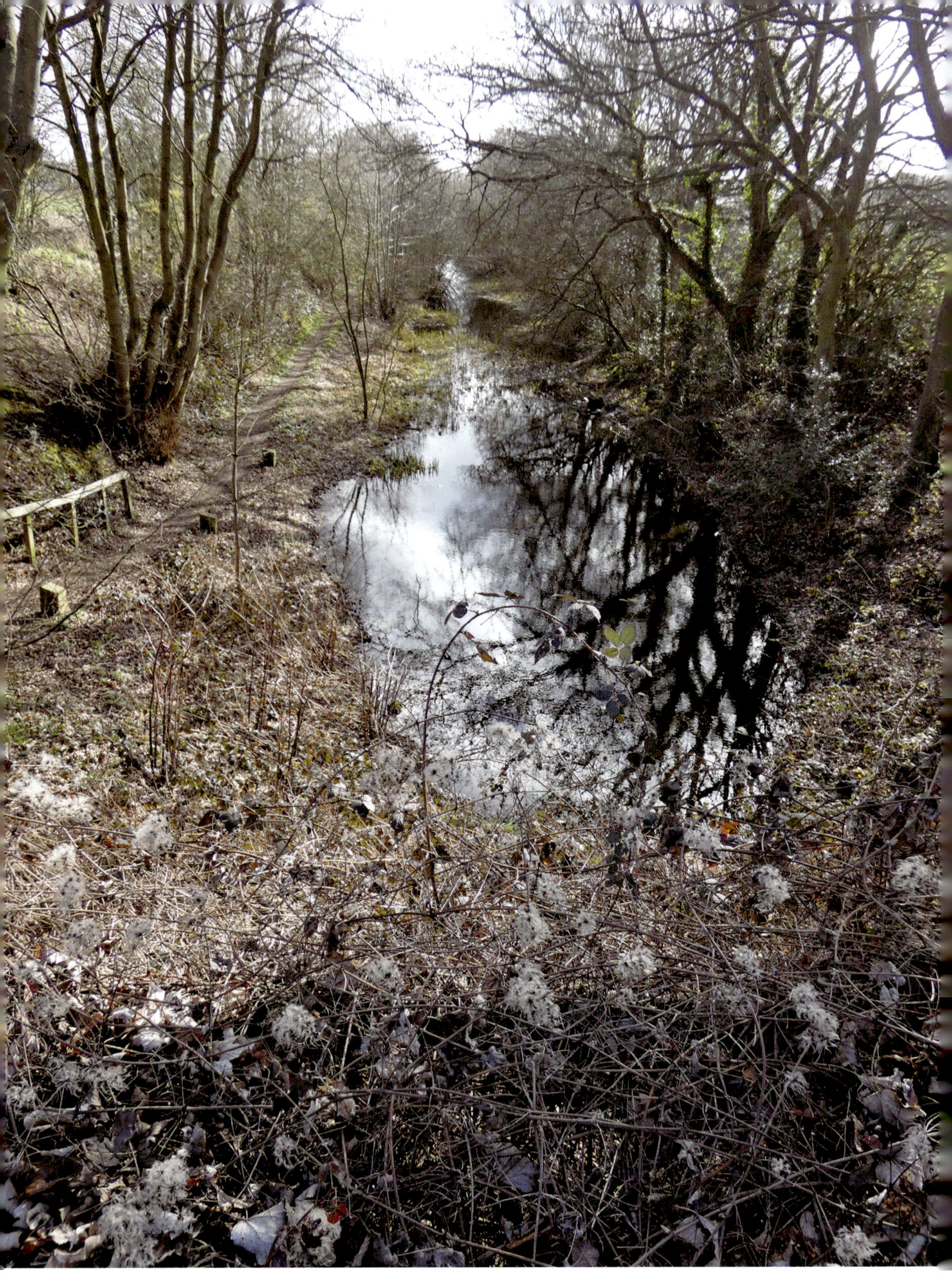

Very much overgrown today, a laden boat would not have the water depth to move a boat.

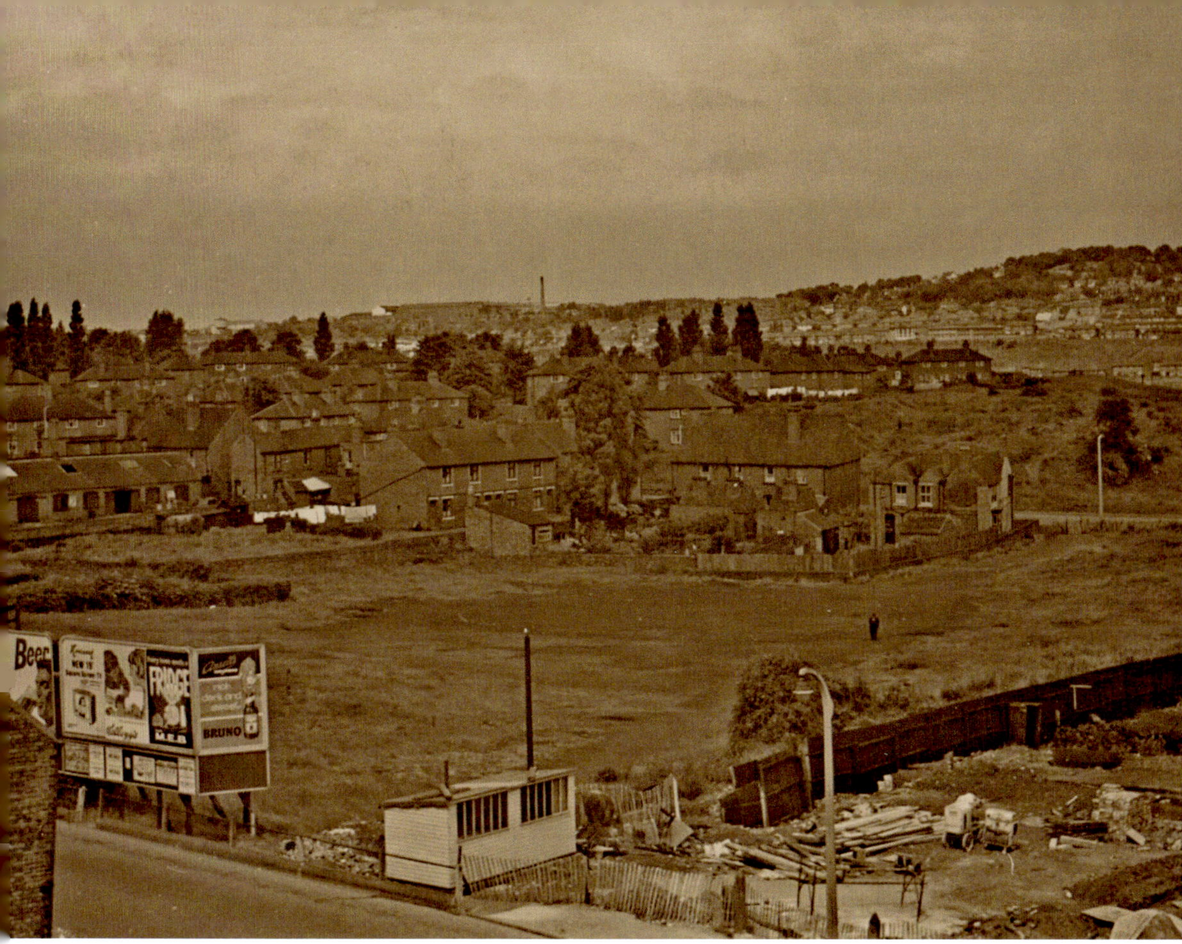

Netherton Fairground and public footpath. Taken from a refuse bank of a disused coal mine, looking across Halesowen Road to Northfield Road. (Ref: pst/1370, courtesy of Dudley Archives and Local History Service)

By opening the stop gates this allowed the head of water to flow back into the canal and, much like a surfer rides a wave, gave the boat(s) a push through the tunnel. Although this reduced the strain on the backs of those legging or polling through the tunnel, it hardly accelerated the boat at all and still resulted in a journey time of three hours through the tunnel.

Lapal Tunnel suffered many collapses during its working life. Eventually, due to mining subsidence in 1917, this tunnel was abandoned. Several stretches of the canal and/or tunnel can still be traced, particularly those under the district of Lapal, near Junction 3 of the M5 motorway, and beneath the Woodgate Valley Country Park. Sections between Halesowen and Selly Oak in Birmingham have been filled in, being considered unsafe, and a short un-navigable length can be found in the grounds of the Leasowes, now forming a part of the public park and a golf course.

Restoration of the Lapal Tunnel had been proposed but, after a study of the area in 2007 revealed it would never prove feasible, the idea was abandoned, and focus turned to the replacing the tunnel with a series of locks to take the canal up and over the rise. Costs for this ambitious project mean it is unlikely to happen in the foreseeable future and thus, in the meantime the Lapal Canal Trust have turned their attention to restoring parts of the Dudley No. 2 Canal to make them navigable to the tunnel entrance sites at Halesowen from Hawne Basin.

7

GOSTY HILL TUNNEL

Hawne Basin, as mentioned in the previous chapter on the Lapal Tunnel, is to the north of Halesowen and near where Gosty Hill Tunnel was constructed. Dudley No. 2 Canal disappears under Gosty Hill between Smiths Bridge and Wrights Bridge near Old Hill Station, running south-east for 557 yards to emerge near Coombswood Way. While much shorter, the bore of 7 feet 9 inches and 6 feet clearance above the water are identical for some of the route.

Boaters of old often commented on how slow their progress would be inside the tunnel. This not just a result of the narrow width but also due to the tunnel often silting up. Leaving the engine running, these boaters would retire to their cabin and make a cup of tea during their passage. Today boaters report equally slow progress.

Among the less useful scrawl at this end of Gosty Hill Tunnel is the modern sign which indicates its length, and at the top of the arch is the date of construction – 1881.

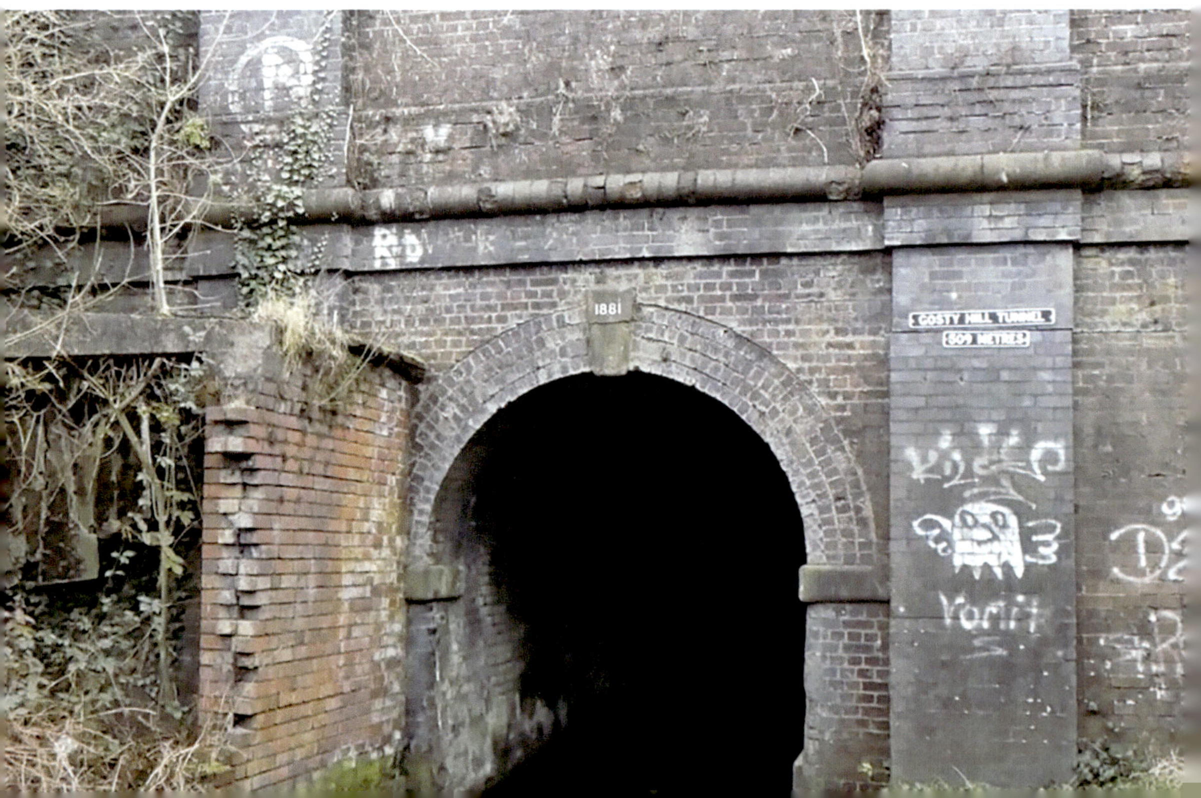

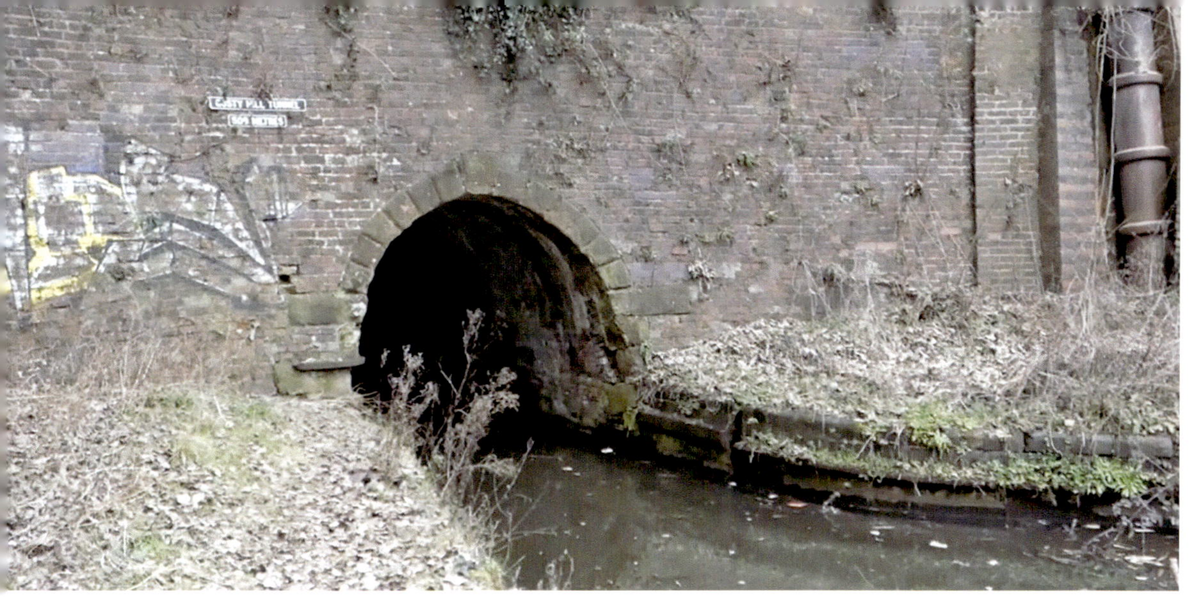

Above: The other end of Gosty Tunnel also has its share of graffiti.

Right: The lines emerge from Old Hill railway tunnel.

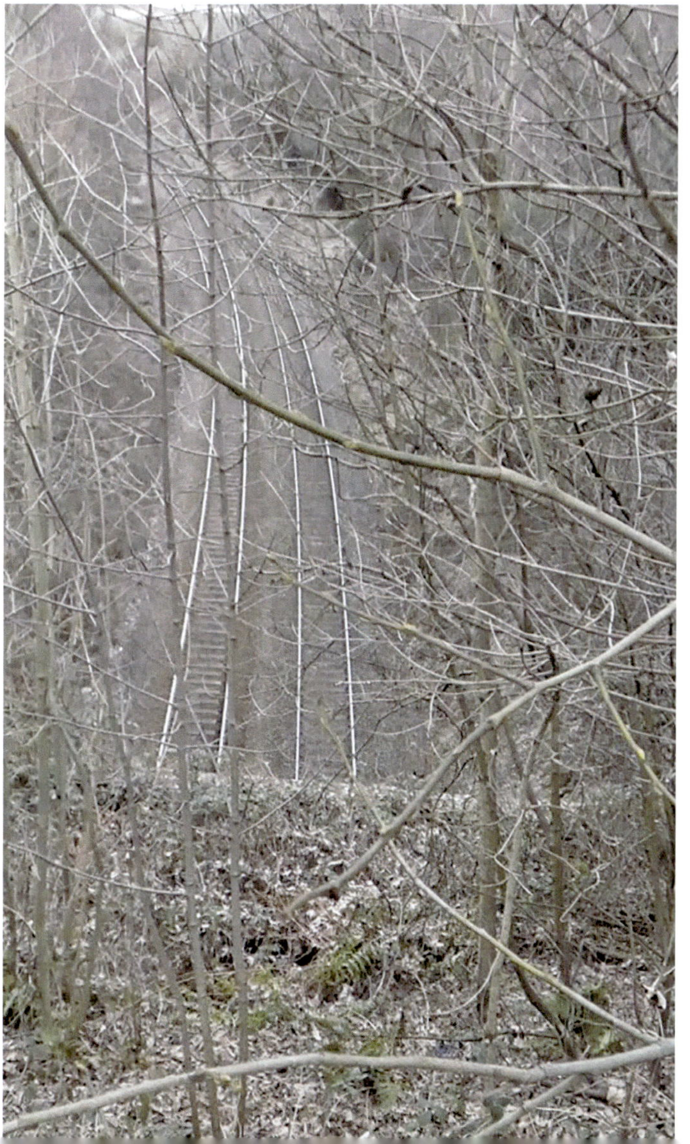

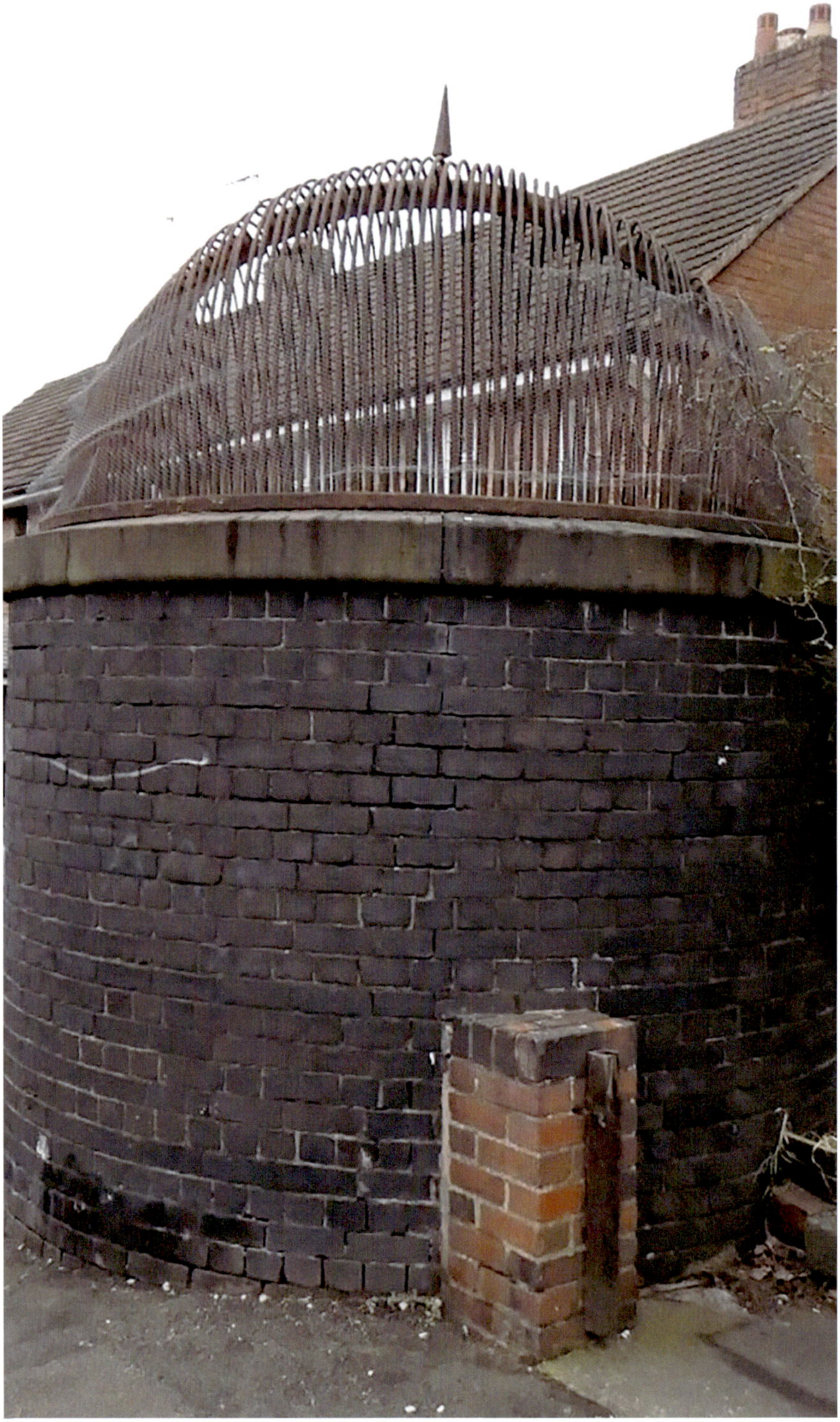

Gosty Hill Tunnel ventilation shaft.

Unlike Lapal Tunnel, Gosty Hill is not of equal height throughout. The low ceiling only appears after about 200 yards after entering from the north; a claustrophobic 150 yards further and the ceiling rises once more, only to drop down once again for the final 50 yards before emerging into Hawne Basin. One twenty-first-century boatman reported it taking 21 minutes to complete the journey, as any attempt to drive the engine further simply results in the boat digging itself into the silt on the bottom. Much better to allow the engine to tick over and glide over the silt at a speed of just under one mile per hour.

One strange image down here, just as the tunnel's ceiling dips for the first time when coming from the northern end, is an image which looks very much like Count Dracula painted on the wall facing. It is not clear whether this is the reason for the ghost story, or whether the tale predates the image, but there is the oft-told tale of a ghost which is said to haunt this dark and gloomy passage.

Versions differ somewhat, but the general theme concerns a couple of boaters who were having engine problems whilst within the tunnel and travelling south. When the engine stalled the two friends were forced to leg it through the remainder. Mooring up, one man with the skills opts to tackle the engine, while the second takes a walk and examines what remains of the former Stewarts and Lloyds Steelworks. By the time the second man returned, his friend had long repaired the engine and it was already getting dark. Without saying a word, the wanderer dropped back into the boat and the pair took the boat back into the tunnel on the return journey. Before long the engine seized up again and, with a few curses, the failed engineer gets in position to start legging again. His friend soon joins him and is striding out so fast the first man can scarce catch up. If the engineer had had the breath, he might have asked what on earth his friend had been doing as he smelled as if he had been wading through raw sewage. On emerging at the other end he saw his friend on the towpath. He had taken the route used by the canal horses over the hill, a much quicker route than legging through, and when the boat emerged shouted out, 'What's the idea, abandoning your crew like that?' Turning to see who had helped him leg it through the tunnel, he realised the man, and the smell, had vanished.

One nearby tunnel, at Halesowen, appears to have been planned but never happened. On a map dated 1830, a tunnel measuring 39 yards cuts through a spur of the same hill. It seems the map was produced before the work could be started, never mind completed, for the short-lived alternative seems to have been a shallow cutting and a bridge – if we are reading the industrial archaeology correctly.

8

COSELEY TUNNEL

Coseley Tunnel, which opened in 1837, is just 360 yards long and runs from the northern entrance at Ivyhouse Lane to the south portal in School Street. Both constructions at either end are Grade II listed and are sufficiently wide to permit the boats to pass in both directions and the inclusion of towpaths on both sides.

For such a short stretch of canal, and tunnel, the project's beginning is an interesting story. Coseley Tunnel and its canal added no new destination to the network, the route had been covered by the Birmingham to Wolverhampton Canal, cut between 1769 and 1772. The work of engineer James Brindley, it follows the natural contours of the land to avoid the construction of locks wherever possible. Coseley's canal, the work of engineer Thomas Telford, improved the route by taking a straight line. Telford originally suggested putting a deep cutting through Coseley, but thankfully this was dismissed as impractical as it would split the town in two, thus the tunnel option was chosen. This cutting versus tunnel debate proved so drawn out that while the approaches to the tunnel had been completed by 1829, the cutting of the tunnel did not start (and finish) until 1835, and still it took another two years for the first traffic to come through here. Not only is the route straight, and therefore faster, but is also 7 miles shorter – well worth the wait.

A clear view through Coseley Tunnel…

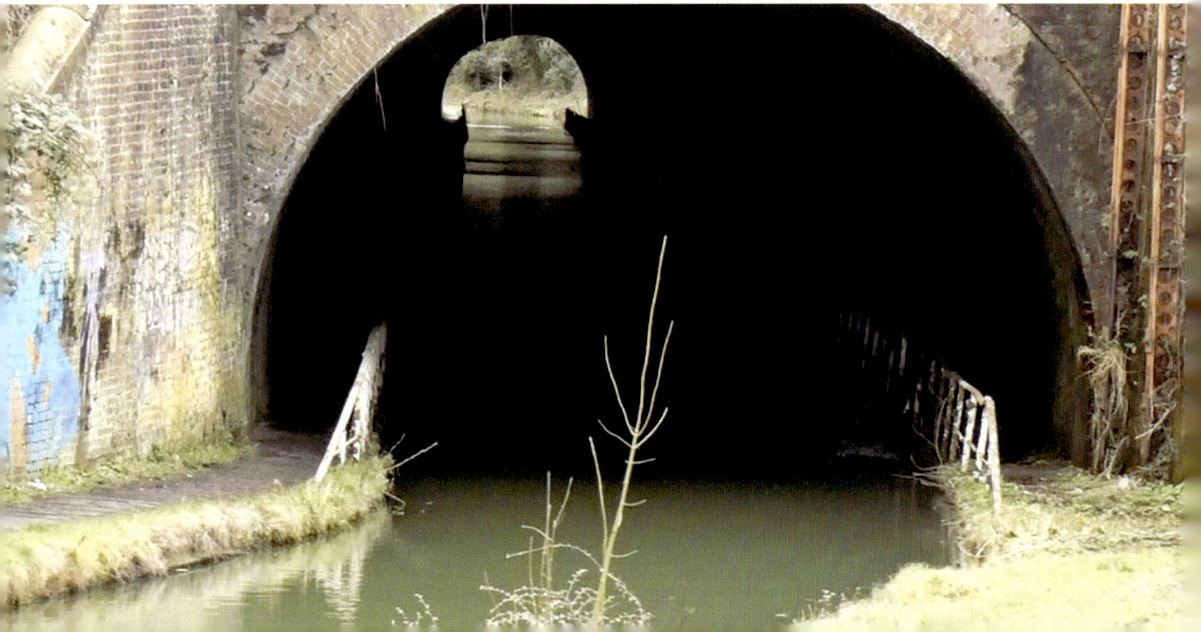

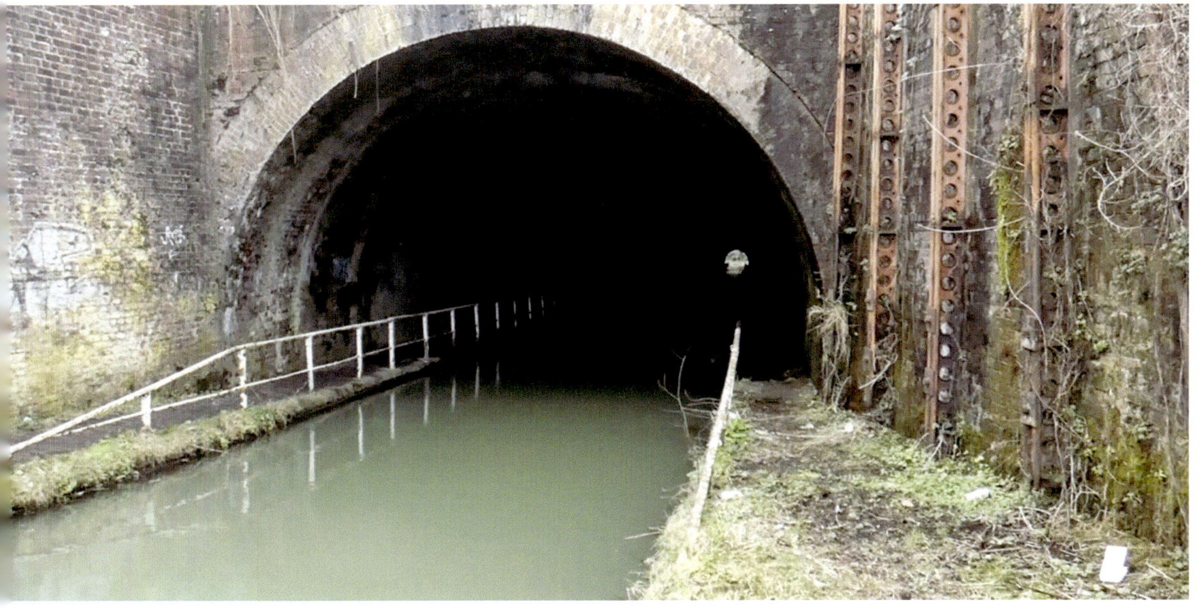

...and Coseley Tunnel from the opposite end.

9

DUDLEY RAILWAY TUNNEL

This tunnel opened in 1850 and ran between railway stations at Dudley and Blowers Green. Wide enough to allow two tracks to pass through, this was part of the Oxford, Worcester, and Wolverhampton line which, almost from its conception, quickly became known by the rather unkind acronym as the 'Old Worse and Worse'. What became Blowers Green Station had begun life as Woodside and Netherton in the planning stage, for these were the communities the station would serve. Shortly after opening in 1878 the station's name was Dudley Southside and Netherton, and not until 1921 was it renamed Blowers Green.

Within a few short years of the opening of what would become Blowers Green, passenger numbers were already in decline, and by 1887 the line served mostly freight. Dudley, however, could boast reasonable numbers for most of its existence. The frequent services made it popular with locals and the station saw good numbers coming through here until the 1950s. Yet it was the lack of numbers on other stations along the line which led to the line closing in 1964, a victim of the so-called Beeching Axe. Dudley Station remained open until 1967, being used for parcels until demolished to make way for the ground-breaking Dudley Freightliner Terminal.

The Old Mitre public house was the only visible reminder of the colliery of the same name. Now that has gone too.

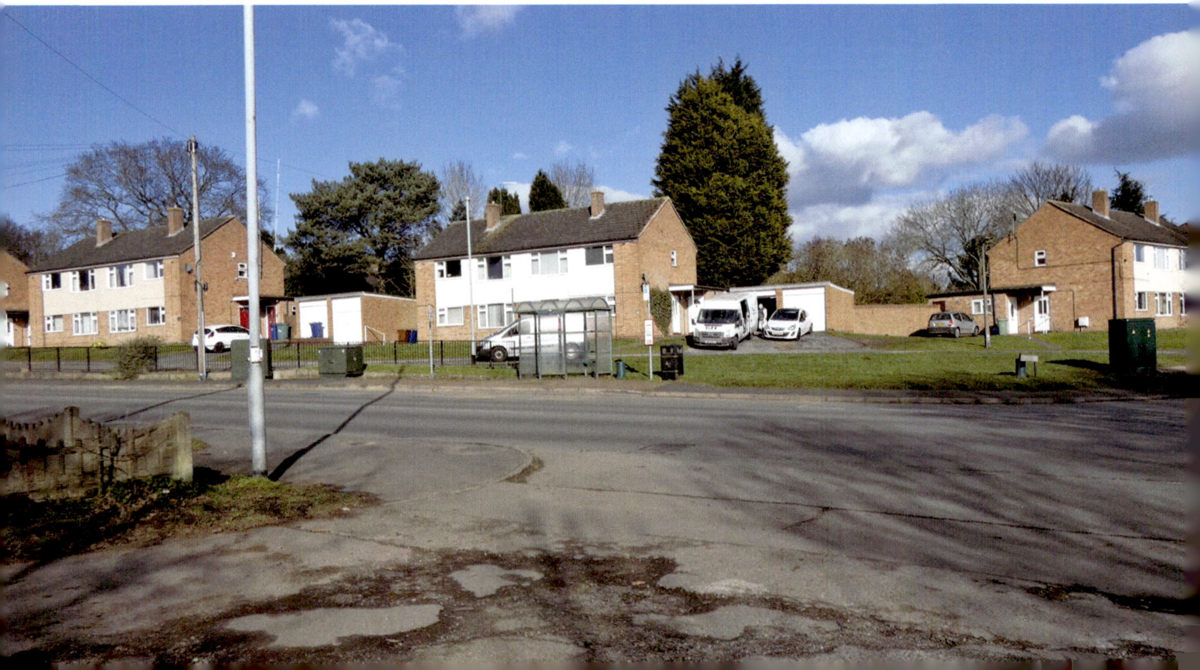

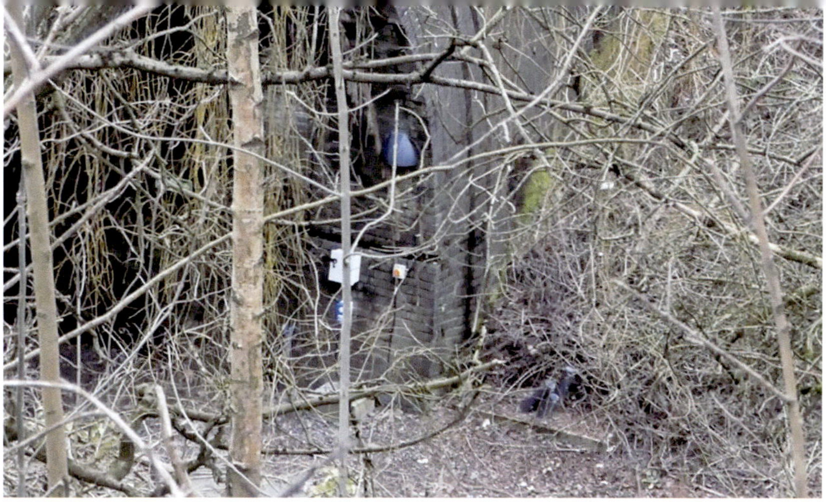

Above: Very much overgrown today, Dudley railway tunnel is just about visible.

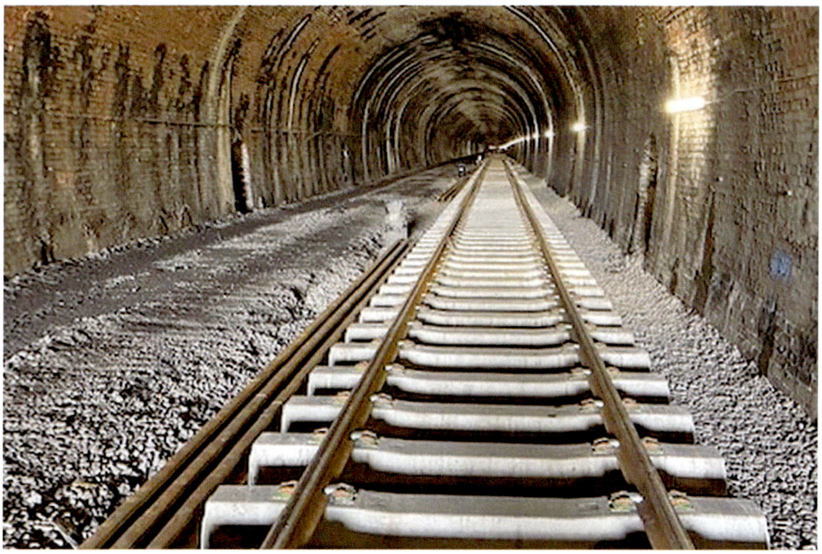

Birmingham mail tunnel between Castle Gate and Cinder Bank.

Between these two stations stands Dudley Railway Tunnel. Few railway tunnels in the country can have had such a chequered story. Indeed, had it not been for the terrain making the construction of a railway line well-nigh impossible to contemplate without it, the tunnel may never have been built. Whether carrying passengers or the more common freight trains, the tunnel remained in use for commuters until the axe fell in 1964, with trains still being sent through the tunnel until as recently as 19 March 1993, when the line closed, seemingly forever. It seems nobody bothered to close it off completely, for a cable laying train came through the tunnel on 1 July 1993, 104 days after the tunnel had been officially closed.

In the twenty-first century the tunnel will get a new lease of life. It will not feature on the extension to the West Midlands Metro, albeit that light rail or tram system will utilise much of the track bed of the earlier line – the gauge will also permit use by freight trains once more. The tunnel has found a new life as a test site for the Very Light Rail National Innovation Centre. At 2 kilometres in length, the tunnel runs between Castle Gate and Cinder Bank, will have a test passenger platform at Cinder Bank, and the centre's hub at the site of the former Dudley Station. Featuring an engineering hall, conference facilities, an auditorium, exhibition space, and offices for almost fifty people.

10

OLD HILL RAILWAY TUNNEL

Completed in 1867, the 896 yards that is the Old Hill Tunnel took rail traffic beneath Rowley Regis on the Stourbridge to Birmingham Snow Hill line. Connected by a short railway line of just 3 miles known as the Bumble Hole Line, this former track bed has no tunnel itself, but once linked the Old Hill Tunnel with Dudley Tunnel. This typical branch line featured five intermediate points: the stations of Baptist End, Windmill End, Darby End, and Old Hill High Street, together with Withymoor Goods Yard.

It is the station of Windmill End which epitomises the problems of the traditional branch line. When it closed in 1964 due to the Beeching Axe – freight continuing until January 1968 – Windmill End featured as the last mentioned in the song 'Slow Train' by Michael Flanders and Donald Swann. While the comic duo may have bemoaned its closure, perhaps Dr Beeching had a point, for records clearly show the line was operated by a single-car Class 122 DMU and Windmill End Station saw just one person using it per day over several years.

Unlike the Dudley Tunnel nearby, Old Hill Tunnel had a £2 million facelift in early 2020. The work, part of a national scheme to upgrade railway structures, many of which, like Old Hill Tunnel, were built in the Victorian era, involved strengthening, repairing brickwork, updating the lining, and ensuring the tunnel was waterproofed once more. In the twenty-first century the tunnel got a new lease of life. This involved closing the tunnel to traffic for six consecutive Sundays. While the workers were inside air quality had to be monitored, with temporary forced ventilation installed. With no storage in the tunnel, all equipment had to be brought in each week and, after the shift had been completed, everything had to be removed once more.

The tunnel will not feature on the extension to the West Midlands Metro, albeit that light rail or tram system will utilise much of the track bed of the earlier line – the gauge will also permit use by freight trains once more. The tunnel has found a new life as a test site for the Very Light Rail National Innovation Centre. At 2 kilometres in length, the tunnel runs between Castle Gate and Cinder Bank, will have a test passenger platform at Cinder Bank, and the centre's hub at the site of the former Dudley Station. It will feature an engineering hall, conference facilities, an auditorium, exhibition space, and offices for almost fifty people.

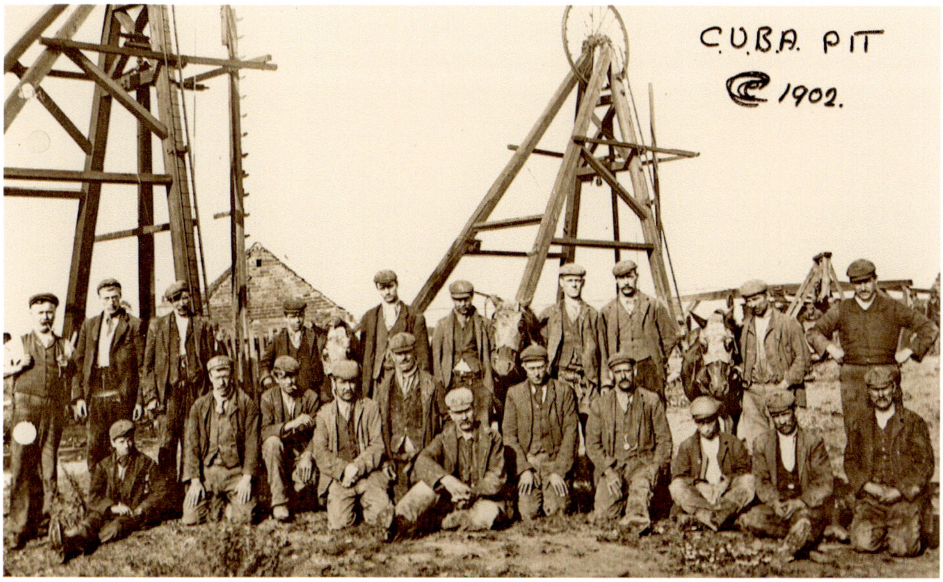

Above: This image shows a group of miners at the pit in front of the wooden winding gear. One of the towers has wooden struts and a ladder, which would most likely be for a person to climb up for maintenance purposes. The use of horses as shown illustrates just how important they were in the running of the mine, particularly when transporting the coal. (Ref: p/1859, courtesy of Dudley Archives and Local History Service)

Below: Toll End canal bridge over the Dudley No. 2 Canal at Bumble Hole between St Peter's Road and the Netherton Tunnel. It was so called because it was made at Horseley Ironworks near Toll End, Tipton. The arched bridge has a distinctive pattern on the sides. The makers of the bridge can also be clearly seen on the side. On the opposite canal bank are what appear to be workers either loading or unloading a canal barge with coal. The way the boat is lying deep in the water suggests that it is heavy laden. (Ref: p/2177, courtesy of Dudley Archives and Local History Service)

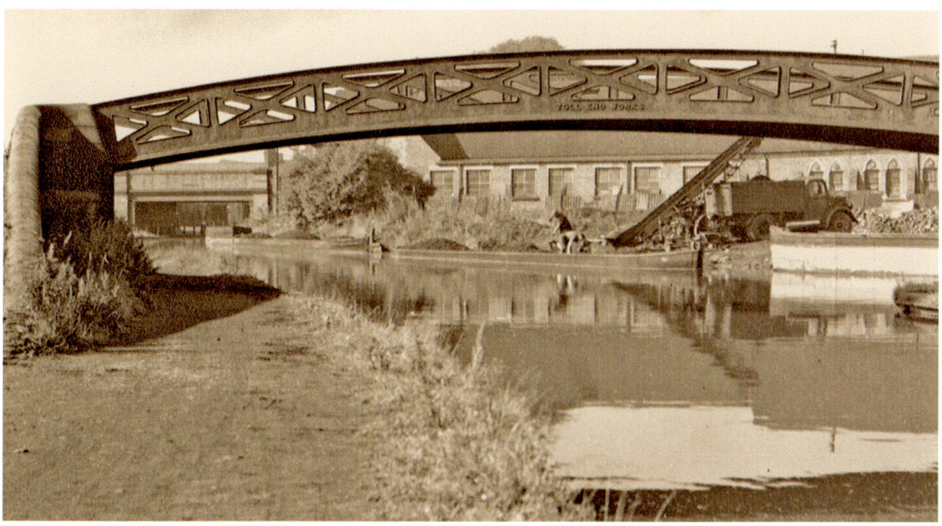

11

PATENT SHAFT ROUNDABOUT TUNNEL

It may seem strange to have a roundabout featured in a volume on what lies underground, but the name is used purely to locate the site. Similarly, it is not by turning to the second element of the name, for this is not a shaft in the underground sense. The name comes from the former steelworks which occupied this site. The Patent Shaft and Axletree Company, established here in 1840, was a major employer in Wednesbury, giving a living to hundreds of workers and their families. A major local player in the Industrial Revolution, the business survived two world wars and numerous economic problems before a decline in manufacturing forced closure in 1980.

While the buildings were demolished in 1983, the gates which had stood alongside the canal towpath for many years and had been saved, were installed at the island in 2010. Meantime, the site changed beyond recognition in the 1990s with the construction of the Black Country Spine Road. Not only did this improve movement of traffic but allowed several square miles of previously inaccessible and unusable land to be utilised for commercial and light industrial ventures, the first major increase in jobs in the area since the Industrial Revolution. This included a (then) unique development in the Component Automotive Park, where every unit was given over to automotive component manufacturers.

In the middle of the roundabout, and with access to the interior closed off, is a railway tunnel which had given access to the Patent Shaft Steelworks right up until its closure.

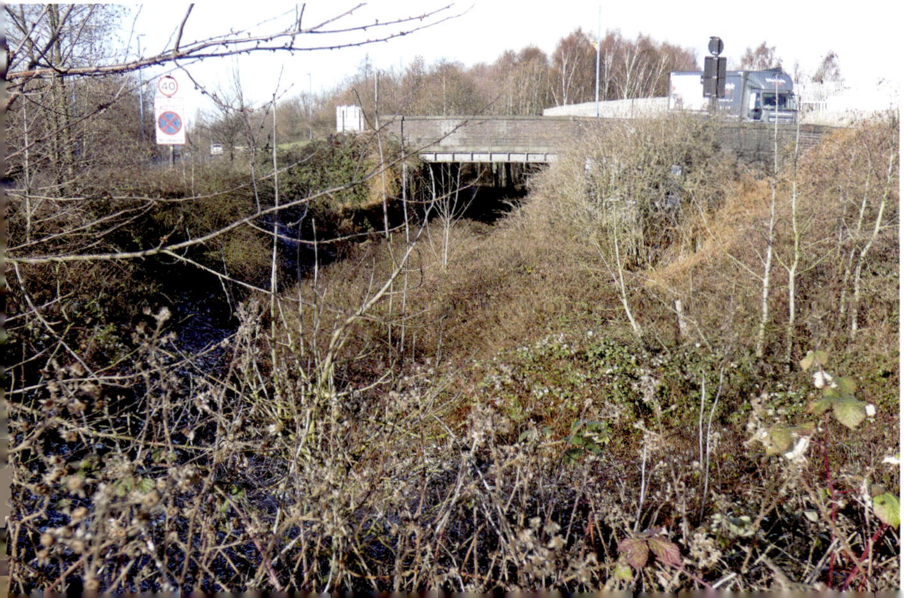

Patent Shaft Roundabout.

12

DUDLEY ZOO CAVERNS

In the previous chapter we headed for a roundabout; in this one, we are off to the bottom of the ocean. Not that global warming has raised sea levels quite this much yet, for this is not a modern sea floor but one dating from 400 million years ago. With tectonic plate movements folding and raising the earth's crust, the fossilised remains from those aeons ago now lie beneath the rise topped by Dudley Castle.

The rock of Silurian limestone had naturally eroded over time before the limestone was quarried – for around a hundred years from approximately 1750. In the earliest times this would have been used for mortar and agriculture, later in the production of iron. This produced caverns up to 390 feet in length, with a ceiling rising 65 feet above the floor. During the First World War the caverns were used by the army for storage, with clothing and ammunition kept here – hence acquiring the name of Stores Cavern. All this well after the first stone-built castle was erected in the twelfth century and before the Earl of Dudley opened the zoo, the public first admitted on 18 May 1937. Whilst none of the exhibits today are listed as 'underground' species, the caverns, and particularly the tunnels, are home to several species of bat, including recent sightings of the rare lesser horseshoe bat.

There are three tunnel openings to the caverns, which is where the bats are normally to be found, and several buildings which would need to be attended to, all of which require extensive studies before these caverns can be opened up as a visitor attraction, which has been planned during the last decade.

13

WREN'S NEST

We are not travelling far from the previous chapter. Indeed, it is only on the other side of the hill from Dudley Castle we find the Seven Sisters and the Wren's Nest. A site of Special Scientific Interest, Wren's Nest is also one of Britain's most important geological locations. It is listed as a local nature reserve, a scheduled ancient monument, is home to several species of birds, a number of rare flora, and a hibernation site for no less than seven different species of bats.

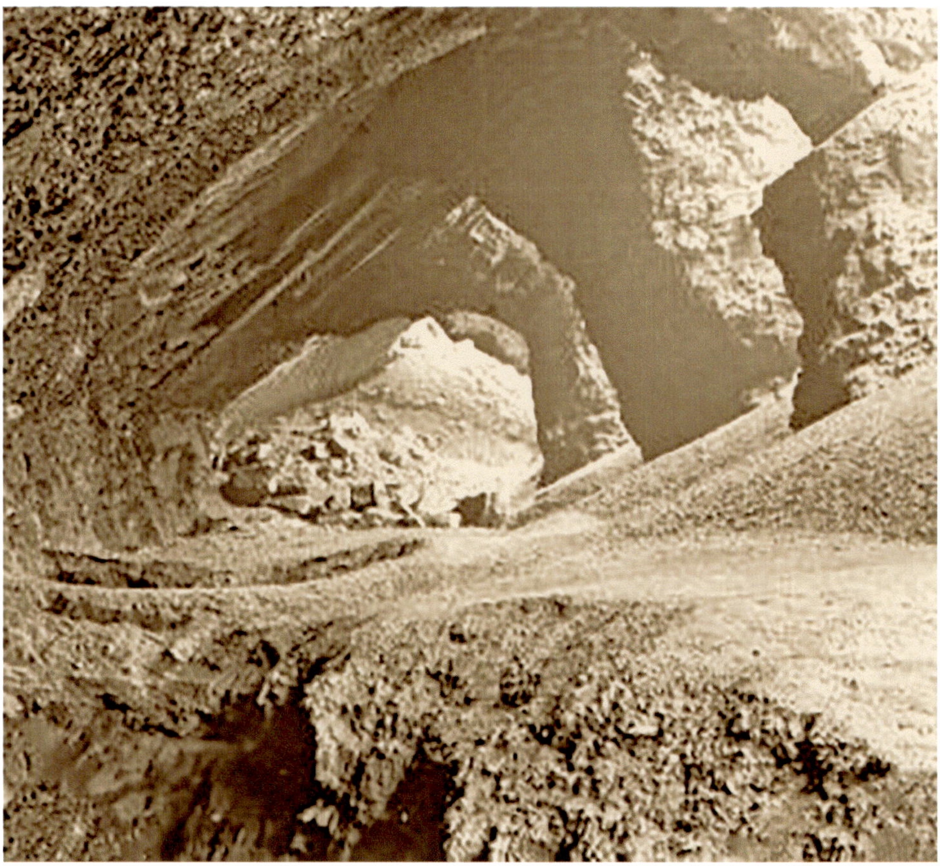

Seven Sister Cavern at Dudley, *c.* 1920. (Courtesy of Sedgley Local History Society)

Geologically, the area is renowned for its Silurian coral reef fossils and ripple marks from the sea's action. Out of more than 700 fossils found at the site, eighty-six are unique to this location. Altogether it provides a record of life on earth as it was some 425 million years ago. Palaeontologist Sir Roderick Murchison made an extensive survey of the area in the 1860s and 1870s. Earlier, the rock had been used for stone building and lime production. During the height of the Industrial Revolution some 20,000 tons of limestone was quarried annually here. Perhaps it even inspired Abraham Darby as one of the leading lights of the early Industrial Revolution, for he was born at Wren's Nest Hill in 1678. In 1925, when quarrying finished, the site was abandoned.

In 1956 Wren's Nest claimed another landmark when becoming the United Kingdom's first national nature reserve for geology. Declared a scheduled ancient monument in 2004, it includes the last remaining surface opening limestone cavern in the world. Once reaching a depth of 330 feet below ground and known as the Seven Sisters, the tunnels once ran right through to the canal tunnels discussed in earlier chapters. Sadly, these tunnels, considered the best example of limestone quarrying still in existence, are showing their age in recent years. A roof collapse and cave-in during 2001 resulted in the tunnels being partially filled to prevent further collapse.

More recently the Cathedral Gallery has been filled with loose sand as Dudley Council try to retain and even redevelop what is claimed as one of the world's most important geological and industrial mining sites. There is certainly the drive and ambition to secure this site for the future. Given time and the resources we can only hope these caverns are accessible to future generations.

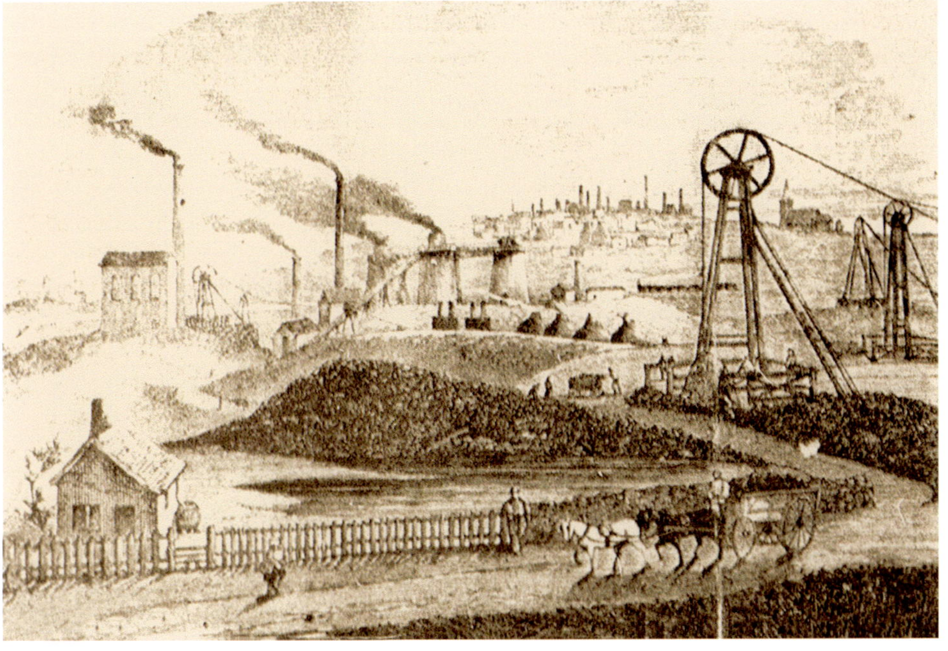

A drawing of a typical pithead blast furnace complex, *c.* 1850. The scene is somewhat stylised and perhaps does not accurately reflect the true environmental impact that coal mining had on the region. The precise location is unknown. (Ref: p/1824, courtesy of Dudley Archives and Local History Service)

14

STATION HOTEL, DUDLEY

A resplendent establishment, one which followed the coming of the railway, opening its doors in May 1898. Despite its name, many guests arrived by carriage, entering at the main entrance on the corner of Trindle Road and Castle Hill, and soon headed for the new Opera House opposite, opening a year later. Inside the hotel the ceiling height reveals the grandeur of those days, albeit what we see today is largely the extensive refurbishment just prior to the Second World War. Thankfully, the broad ornate staircase was retained and is as much of a delight to descend today as it would have been soon after it was first varnished.

Yet our destination lies, as elsewhere in this book, below ground level. Whilst it would be impossible to mention every cellar in the Black Country, these extensive underground passages are more than worthy of mention. These poorly lit, cold, and rather damp rooms connected by equally dark corridors are said to be home to two ghostly figures: a murderer and his victim. The killer is a former manager of the Station Hotel, George Williams (sometimes given as Williamson), reported to be either seen or heard cowering in the corner of the cellar, head in hands, sobbing pitifully. His victim, Elizabeth Hitchen, had been employed as a maid but was also George's mistress. When Elizabeth revealed her pregnancy to George, he proved less than supportive and quite uninterested in her.

Elizabeth, very unimpressed by his reaction, threatened to reveal all to his wife during a particularly vehement confrontation. George fought back, quite literally, stabbing and then strangling the poor woman. He then had to dispose of the body and chose the chute along which barrels were delivered to the cellar. Bringing the full barrels down was simple enough, getting the empties back up involved wrapping a rope around the barrel several times then, by pulling on one end, rolling the barrel up the slope. While the corpse would not roll, it could be dragged up the metal chute at the end of a rope. At the top, he is said to have buried her under a patch of grass at the side of the hotel, one with a significant lump but which has never been shown to contain a body.

No record has been found to suggest George Williams or anyone else has ever been charged or tried for the murder of Elizabeth Hitchen.

15

BAGGERIDGE COLLIERY

In 1889 a test shaft was drilled in Baggeridge Wood, near Sedgley. In October Lord Dudley invested £25,000 in a new coal mining development, which was hoped would enable them to work a thick coal seam extending over an area of more than a thousand acres. Three years later, and with the familiar image of an early twentieth-century mine having appeared on the skyline, the first shaft was sunk to reach the coal seam lying 1,800 feet below ground level. Two more shafts were sunk in 1910, with full production beginning two years later.

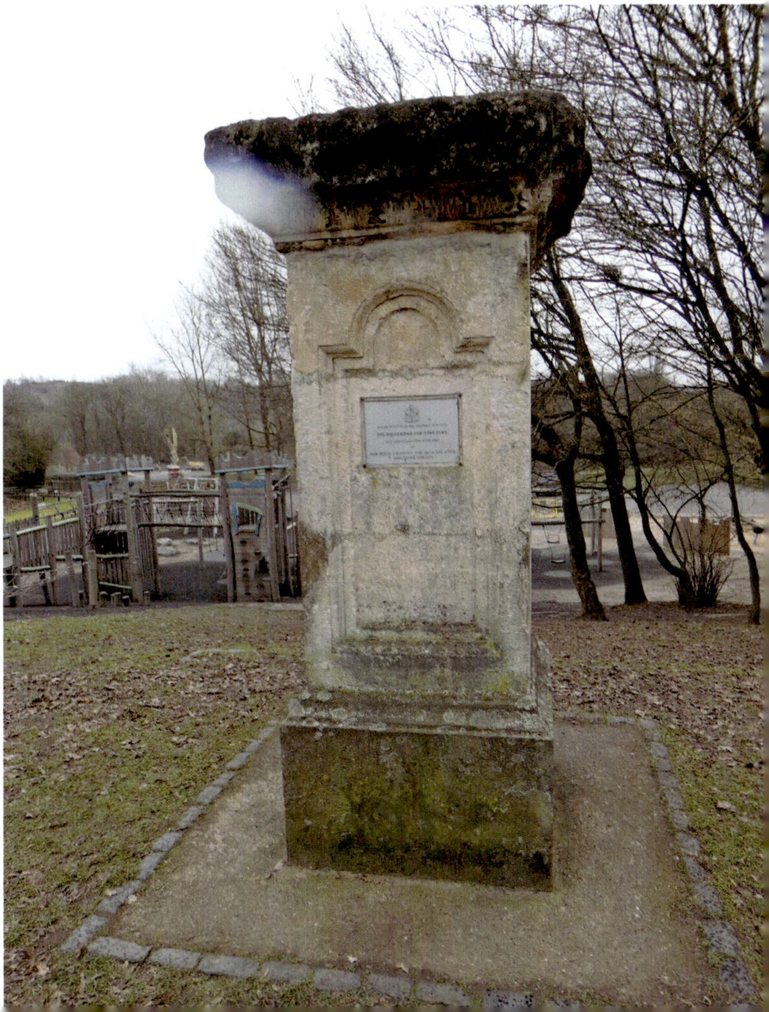

Memorial at Baggeridge Country Park remembering the mine of the same name.

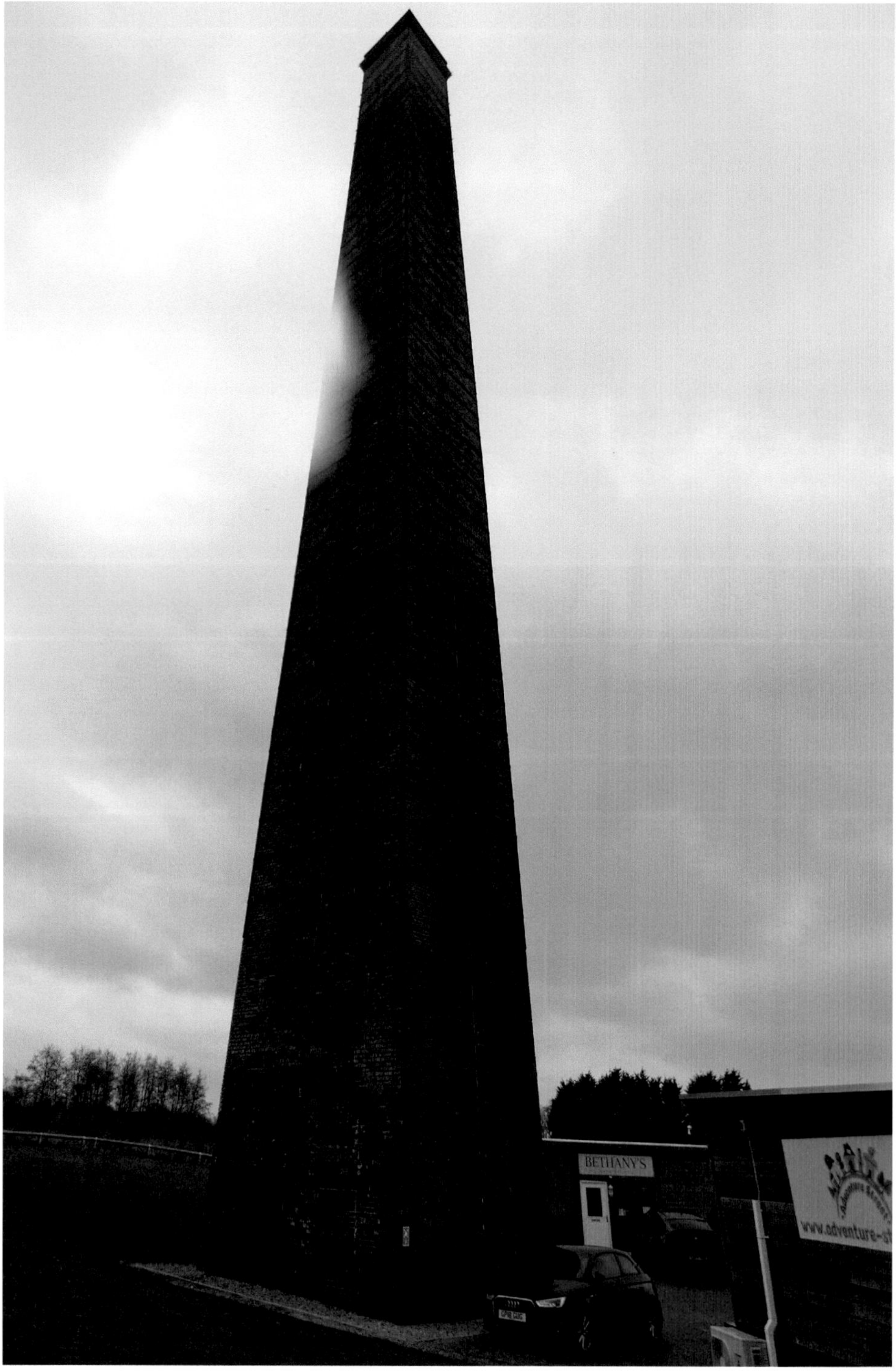

The old chimney at Baggeridge Country Park still stands today overlooking a number of retail outlets.

At its peak the colliery employed 3,000 men, many coming from Gornal, and produced over half a million tons of coal annually. Taken from a seam twenty feet thick and of superior quality, a newspaper report dated 29 January 1907 described the coal seam as 'practically inexhaustible'. While it may have seemed so early in 1907, as we all know extraction methods would improve over time and had to as demand increased. Thus, it will come as no surprise to find the colliery closed on 2 March 1968. This was the last mine to close in the Black Country and, unlike Sedgley which became part of the West Midlands, in the local government reorganisation of 1974 Baggeridge became part of Seisdon and thus remained a part of Staffordshire.

Our interest is in what is underground today, and there is one tell-tale reminder of the former colliery. When the area was landscaped, the 350-acre Baggeridge Country Park being opened on 17 June 1983, a large housing development also grew around it, the tall chimney from the colliery still stood overlooking the area. There are four pools in the park, set aside for coarse fishing.

The face of a coal seam, *c.* 1930. Wooden pit props hold up the roof. The type of coal in the picture is called 'brooch' coal. (Ref: p/1880, courtesy of Dudley Archives and Local History Service)

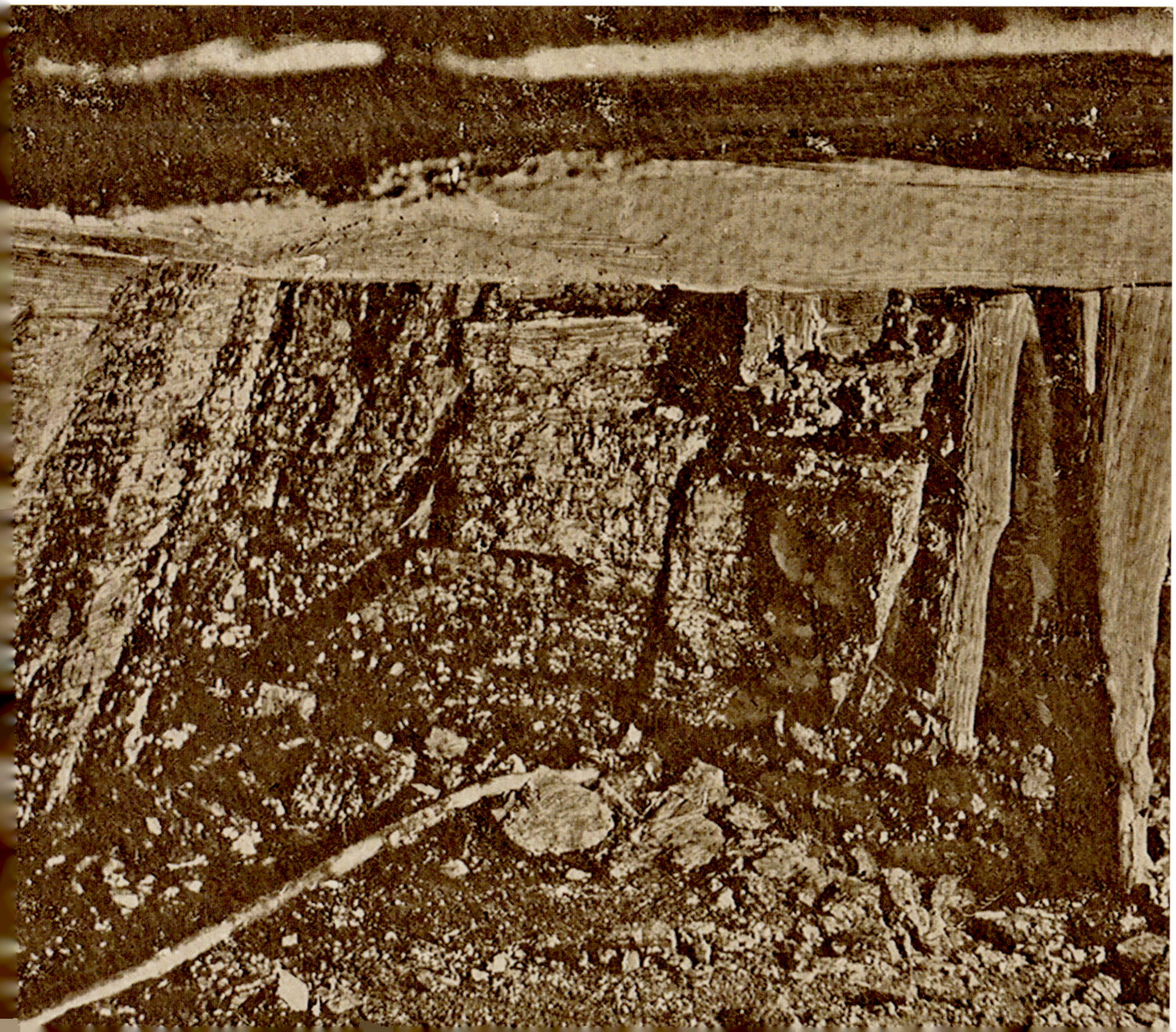

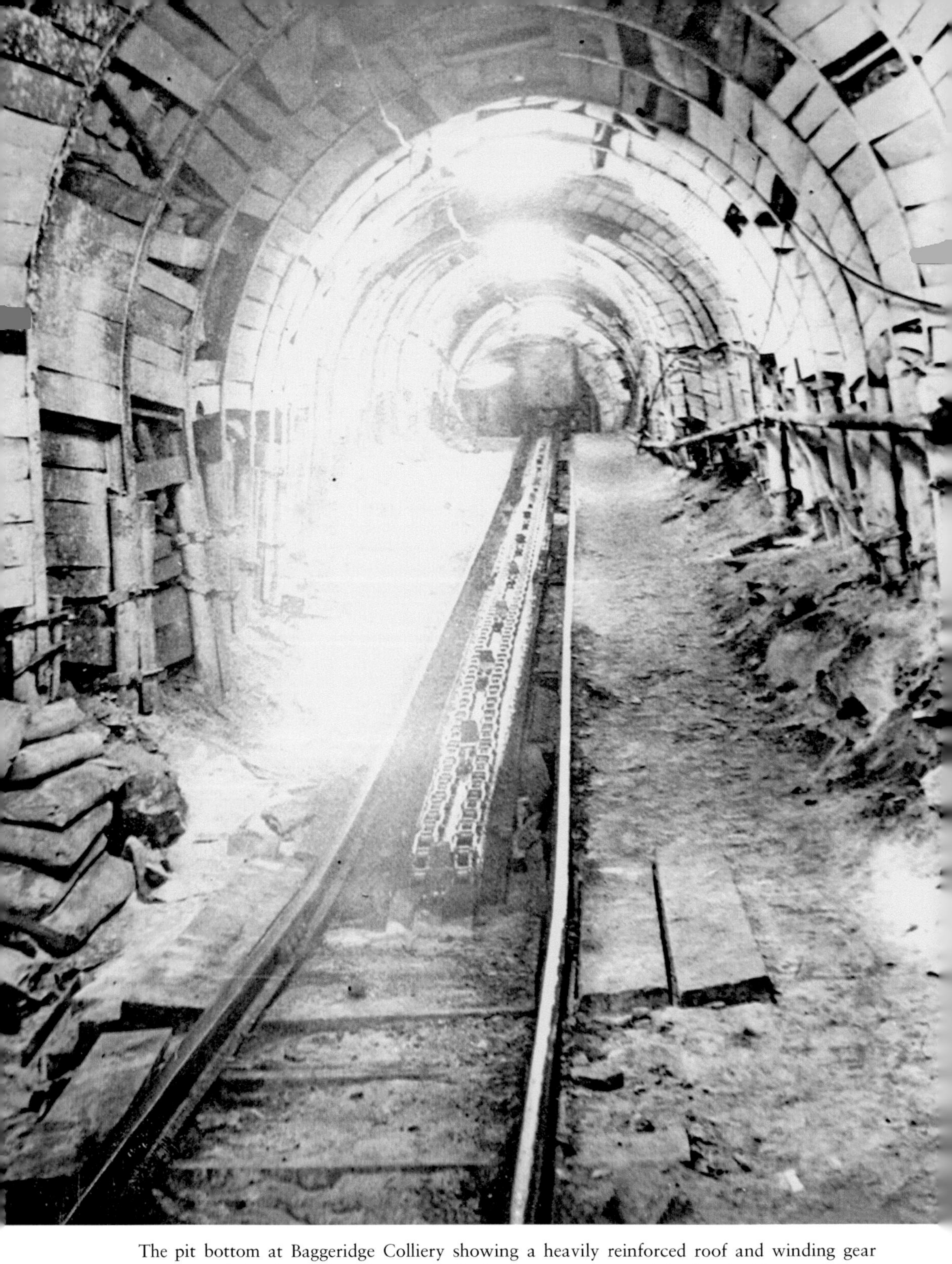

The pit bottom at Baggeridge Colliery showing a heavily reinforced roof and winding gear on the track for the coal trucks, 1960s. (Ref: p/1773, courtesy of Dudley Archives and Local History Service)

16

BROWNHILLS COLLIERY

During the seventeenth century, Brownhills played host to several small-scale shallow coal mine workings. Not until the coming of the Wyrley and Essington Canal in 1797 (known locally as the Curly Wyrley), and particularly the South Staffordshire Railway fifty years later, did we see a huge expansion in mining and, along with it, a veritable explosion in population.

One date which will live in the memory is January 1861. When four men and two boys were working the Red Pit, the signal came at three in the morning to lower the cage and bring them to the surface. On retrieving the cage it was found to be empty, with smoke seen coming from the shaft. By entering through another access, half-a-mile away, they were able to access the seam and found the bodies of all six. In attempting to escape the smoke and fumes, they had inadvertently followed the route taken by the deadly atmosphere being circulated around the shafts by the very pumps intended to keep them supplied with fresh air. So thick was the smoke that a layer of soot had blackened the timber supports in the shafts. Six horses inside the pit were also suffocated while still in their stables.

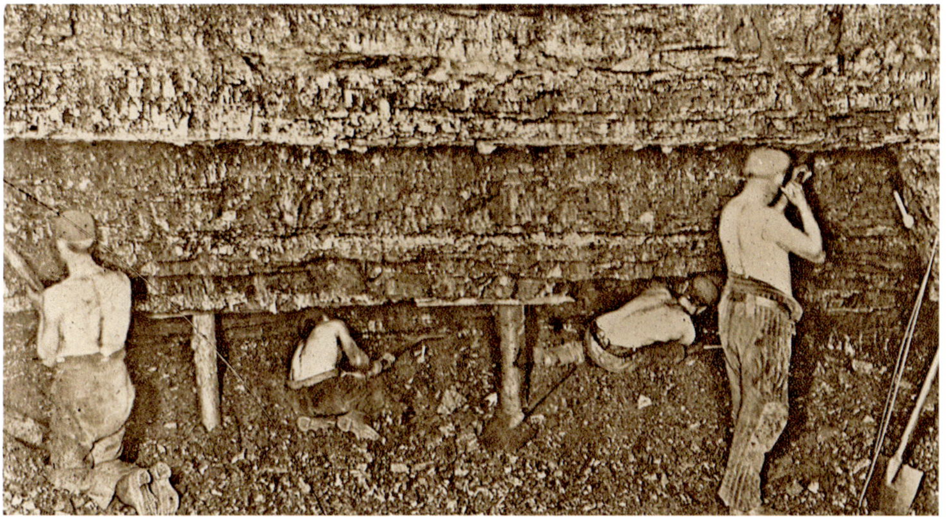

Four miners digging for coal. Two of them are directly beneath the thick coal seam. Note the wooden pit props holding up the seam. The miner on the right is boring a hole for dynamite to be placed prior to blasting. The precise location is unknown. (Ref: p/1814, courtesy of Dudley Archives and Local History Service)

17

CANNOCK CHASE COALFIELD

Whilst other areas are covered under chapters looking at specific collieries, the Cannock Chase Coalfield requires a rather different viewpoint. An extensive area, which not always falls within the area known as the Black Country, worked through many shafts at several pits, features seams running much deeper than those elsewhere in the South Staffordshire Coalfield. The latter lie eight hundred feet down, while the Cannock Chase field is twice that depth. Undoubtedly both were laid down at the same time but geological upheaval over millions of years resulted in the different depths. This separation known as the Bentley Fault.

Some will undoubtedly argue those mines around the Chase are not part of the Black Country. Would this be a book on the overground of the region, I could only agree. However, as the title tells us, this book looks at underground, and there the boundaries above ground have no meaning beneath the surface. Furthermore, the seams worked are all from the same field, and thus are connected. Theoretically, were the seams worked out completely, all the mines above ground would be connected beneath. Indeed, they were undoubtedly connected in terms of workforce, transport, and even ownership above ground, and thus I make no apologies for including these in this book.

Cannock Chase Colliery Company, founded in 1859, produced 3 million tons of coal annually thirty years later. By 1933, this figure had risen to over 5 million tons annually. This impressive tonnage came from more than a dozen pits, several of which were known under different names as they began as individual mines but, as time passed and the networks of workings grew, became linked deep underground.

Cannock Old Coppice opened in 1840 and, before its closure in April 1960, raised many thousands of tons of coal to the surface, employing around a thousand individuals, more than three-quarters underground. For most of its history the pit was under the control of the Hawkins family, at least since being purchased by Joseph Hawkins in 1869, which is why it has more often been known by the shorter name of the Hawkins Colliery. The family retained control until 1947, only handing over the reins with the nationalisation of the coal industry. Yet they retained possession of the neighbouring clay pit at Longhouse, which became the Longhouse Brick and Tile Works producing more than seven million bricks each year, courtesy of the clay they extracted and mixed with the spoil from this mine.

At Hednesford, the Cannock Wood, Wimblebury and Valley colliery mines were under joint ownership, the three employing a total of between 2,000 and 3,000 individuals at any one time. At the time of nationalisation some 600,000 tons of coal were produced annually.

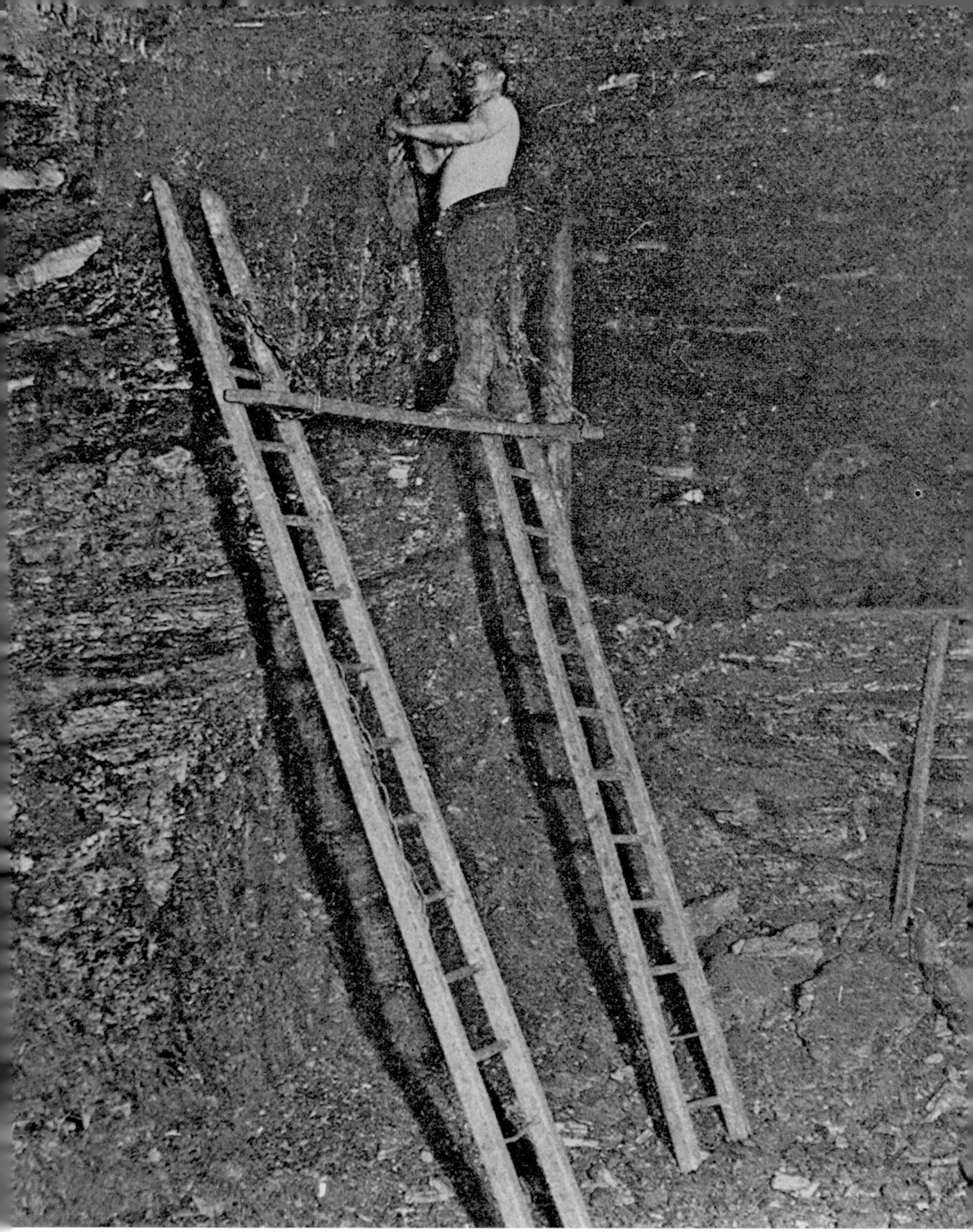

A miner using a pickaxe to hack away at the coal using a crude scaffold made with a plank of wood chained to two ladders. This part of the mine has a layer of thick coal known as the 'ten yard coal'. The precise location is unknown. (Ref: P/1817, courtesy of Dudley Archives and Local History Service)

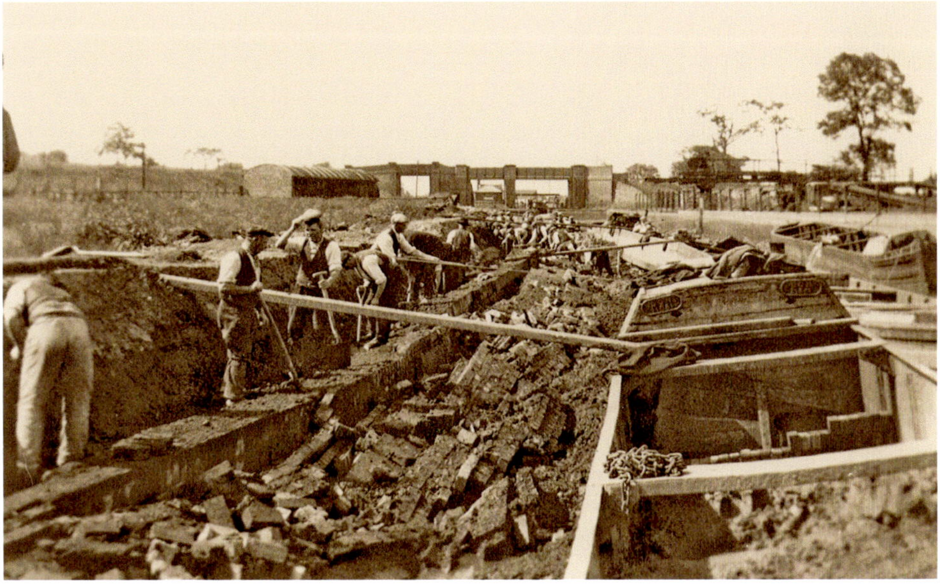

A group of workers who appear to be repairing the side of the Cannock Extension Canal. It appears that part of the left bank of the canal has either fallen in or has been partly demolished for possible repairs. Hednesford Basin (known as 'Edgeford' by the boatmen) was at the end of the Cannock Extension Canal. It was used extensively after the First World War (1914–18) as by this time most of the coal for the Black Country came from Cannock Chase mines. (Ref: p/2034, courtesy of Dudley Archives and Local History Service)

Sinking of shafts at Norton Canes began in 1858, although production only started a few years later. This delay enforced as the ground conditions made sinking shafts troublesome. Conduit Colliery boasted two main pits: No. 3 having three shafts and No. 4, formerly Norton Green Colliery, just two. Both came under the Conduit Colliery Company,until sold to Littleton Collieries in 1930 for £50,000. The colliery closed its doors for the last time in 1962.

Opening in 1893, it took two years to cut through 960 feet down to the twelve coal seams below. For over sixty years Coppice Colliery operated, until closure in 1964. Throughout that time not only coal but the inevitable spoil was also extracted, the latter being dumped on the surrounding heathland. After years of being an eyesore, the former spoil heaps are returning to what nature intended. A patchwork of wetland, heath, and pools supports a wealth of wildlife. Not only the more common varieties, but including the hobby, merlin, blackcap, willow warbler, chiffchaff, snipe, skylark, lapwing, a rare butterfly in the dingy skipper, and a rare plant in the pennyroyal.

Perhaps the most obvious of all the Cannock area coalfields is that of East Cannock. Not that there are any more significant memorials, it is simply that this is home to Chasewater Light Railway and its museum. The reservoir may have opened in 1797, but during the mid-nineteenth century coal seams beneath the reservoir were worked on a large scale. This resulted in the opening of the Anglesey Branch of the Wyrley and Anglesey Canal by 1850, but within a few years problems with sand and gravel came from working too close to an unconsolidated surface forced the colliery to close in January 1857. Undoubtedly those workings are still in existence, albeit today filled with water seeping through from the reservoir together with all the sand and/or gravel washed down with it.

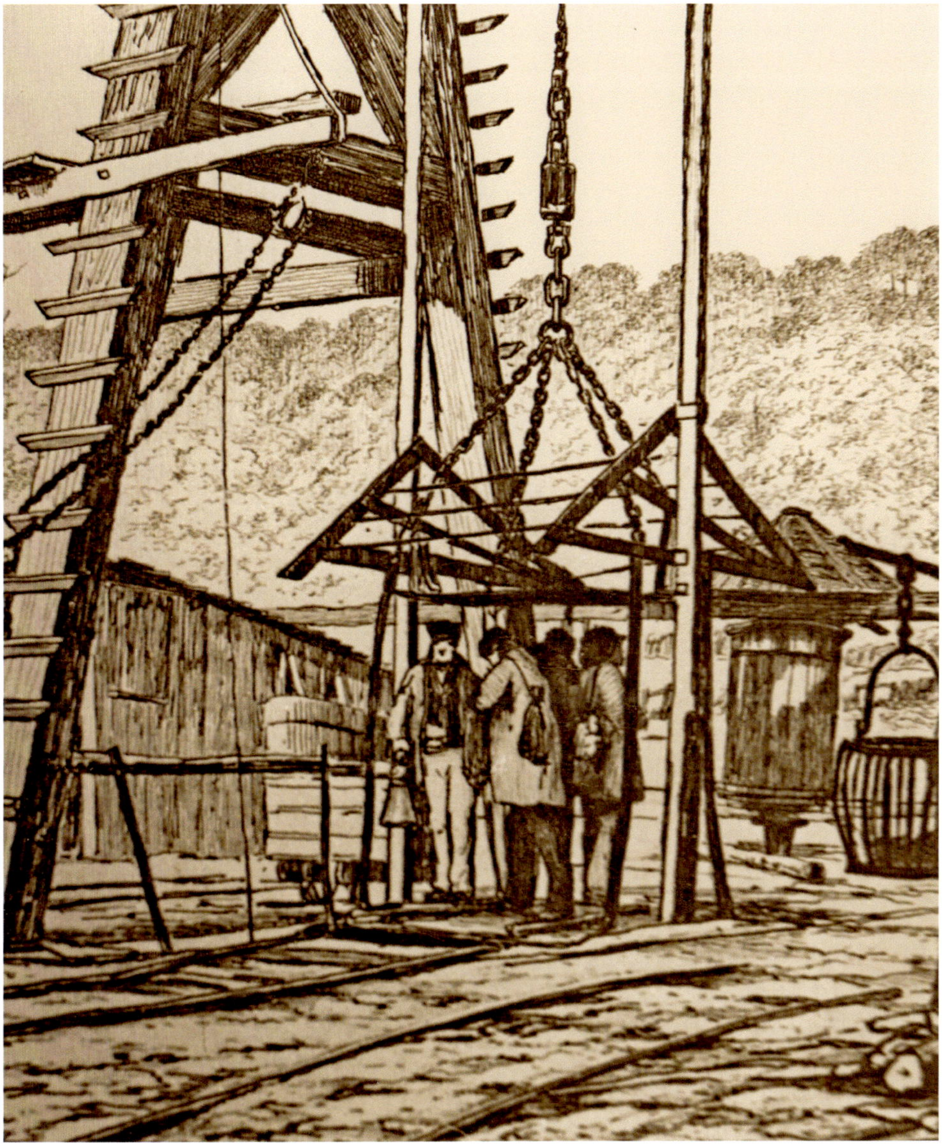

Photograph of an 1872 etching by artist Richard S. Chattock of a pit mouth. It clearly shows the wooden pithead winding gear and wooden miners' conveyance suspended from a chain. The chain moved the conveyance by lifting or lowering it up and down the shaft. The triangular frame above them was called the 'hen-coop' and was placed over the entrance to the mine after the miners had descended, to protect against workers falling down the pit. The miners carry bags, perhaps holding their belongings for the day. The miner on the left appears to be holding some kind of rigid container, possibly for drinks. The contraption to the right of the image is most likely to be a horse gin – it looks like it is meant to be turned round. The large cage-like basket attached to the gin may have been used to hold coal or other equipment. (The original etching was Plate VIII entitled *View of Pit Mouth* from a set of sixteen etchings by the artist on India paper of the coal and iron district of south Staffordshire; Ref: p/1872, courtesy of Dudley Archives and Local History Service)

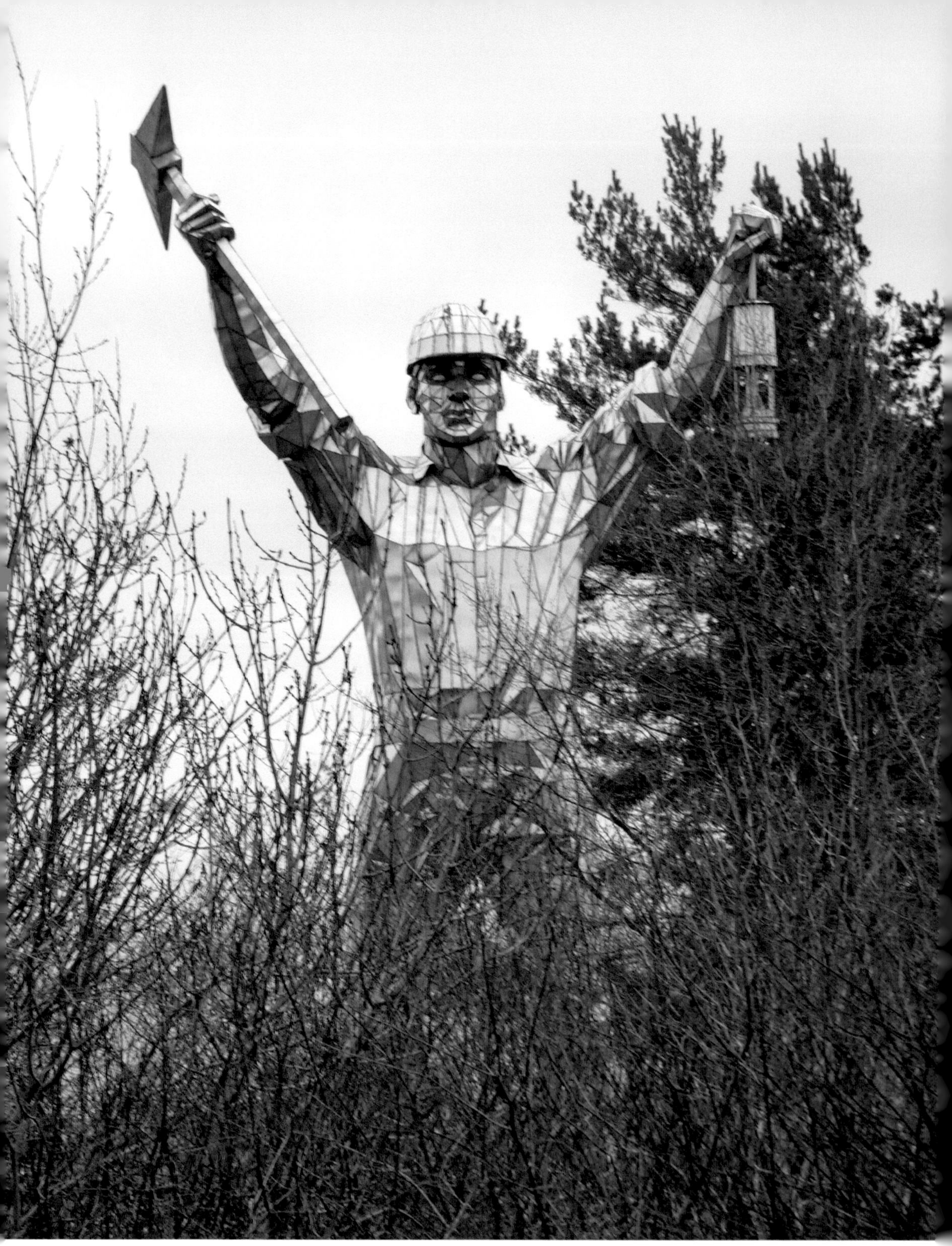

Jack 'Jigger' Taylor's statue at Brownhills, remembering the miner who died when the roof collapsed at Walsall Wood Colliery.

By 1862, Great Wyrley boasted two collieries in operation, the Wyrley New Colliery Company, and the Hatherton Colliery, although coal had been mined here since the early seventeenth century. Ten years later and the Wyrley Cannock Colliery Company had taken the reins, doing so until 1882, and the Great Wyrley Colliery Company operated from 1882 until 1924. Local pits had names such as Fair Oak, Grove, Fair Lady, Nook (Wyrley Cannock No. 1), and Wyrley No. 3, the latter opened by Harrison's Ltd in 1896 and worked until 1956. This company gave the land for the recreation ground in 1921, with the memorial gates listing the men from Great Wyrley who died in the First World War paid for by public subscription.

Wyrley No. 3 was also the scene of a major disaster in 1930. Undoubtedly the darkest day for William Harrison's Brownhills Collieries Company came on the first day of October in 1930. At precisely 9:18 that morning a huge gas explosion rocked the Grove Colliery directly beneath the Fleur de Lys public house. It is thought a naked flame was struck in the shaft. Fourteen men were killed that day, all retrieved from an astonishing 1½ miles beneath the surface. Ten of the men were buried in a collective grave with full military honours, as six had served their country during the First World War.

Norton Colliery and Walsall Wood Colliery were among those served by Norton Junction and its goods yard. Multiple collieries and industrial businesses, particularly Pelsall Steelworks, saw most of their produce come through here, until the decline in coal production during the 1950s saw closure by 1964. At the West Cannock pits, Nos 1, 2, 3, and 5 employed almost 2,000 individuals at the time of nationalisation. West Cannock No. 5 saw, six men die when an explosion through firedamp on 16 May 1933 ripped through the worked seam at a depth of 630 feet and nearly a mile from the shaft.

As pit after pit closed through the years, the last coal was extracted at the Littleton Colliery. With the sinking of the first shaft in 1877, this proved impracticable with a major flooding problem, and the second two years later, so began a colliery producing good amounts of coal until closure 1993. No era proved more productive than those following an upgrade to skip winding in the 1960s, thereafter annual production regularly exceeded 1 million tons.

Complete demolition followed closure, and today only the sheave wheel remains as a memorial to Littleton Colliery. Redevelopment of the area saw the building of a housing development and Littleton Green Community School. Meanwhile, the spoil heap has been landscaped as Littleton Leisure Park.

18

MORE UNDERGROUND WORKINGS ON CANNOCK CHASE

If we were to dedicate a chapter to every coal mine on Cannock Chase, this book would be full of little else. Hence, as with Chapter 17, here we will give but a brief look at the former workings beneath the surface, many of these rather smaller than those in the previous chapter and some have been swallowed by other workings with which they were later connected.

Kingswood Colliery lasted just twenty years, with coal production ceasing in 1959. All above ground traces of the mine have been eradicated, wiped away by the construction of the M6 toll road in the area where it passes beneath the Watling Street.

The Nook Colliery once stood at what is now the end of Dundalk Lane, which sounds rather better than the earlier version of Dun Duck Lane, in what is now a housing estate laid out in the 1980s. One branch of the Wryrley and Essington Canal came alongside the colliery and proved a vital link to the distribution network for the Nook. While mining at the Nook ceased in 1939, surface activity continued until closure on the last day of June 1941.

Just 350 yards southeast of the Nook, and on a bend in Wyrley Branch of the Wyrley and Essington Canal, stood the Dry Bread Colliery. Work here ceased in the 1880s.

A further 660 yards south-east of the Dry Bread Colliery and 440 yards north of Old Landywood Lane could be found Pool Meadow Colliery. This colliery boasted its own canal basin adjacent to the Wyrley and Essington Canal. There are no records as to when this mine closed.

Comprised of two shafts only 35 yards apart, until closure at the end of September 1884 Fishers Farm Colliery stood alongside a point now signed as Upper Landywood Lane and just 150 yards south of Landywood Lane.

The South Cannock Colliery, closing in 1945, stood in the vicinity of South Cannock Farm and accessed from Jacobs Hall Lane. The site can be located by following a line 660 yards east from the junction of the Cannock to Walsall road and Holly Lane in Landywood.

To the south of Cheslyn Hay once stood Spring Meadow Colliery. Closed in 1967, today the location is marked by the line of Upper Landywood Lane where the shaft would have been a landmark along its western edge.

Until it closed in 1960 the Bulls Meadow Colliery burrowed into the ground on the opposite side of Upper Landywood Lane, with other road boundaries coinciding with the modern Landywood Lane and Streets Lane.

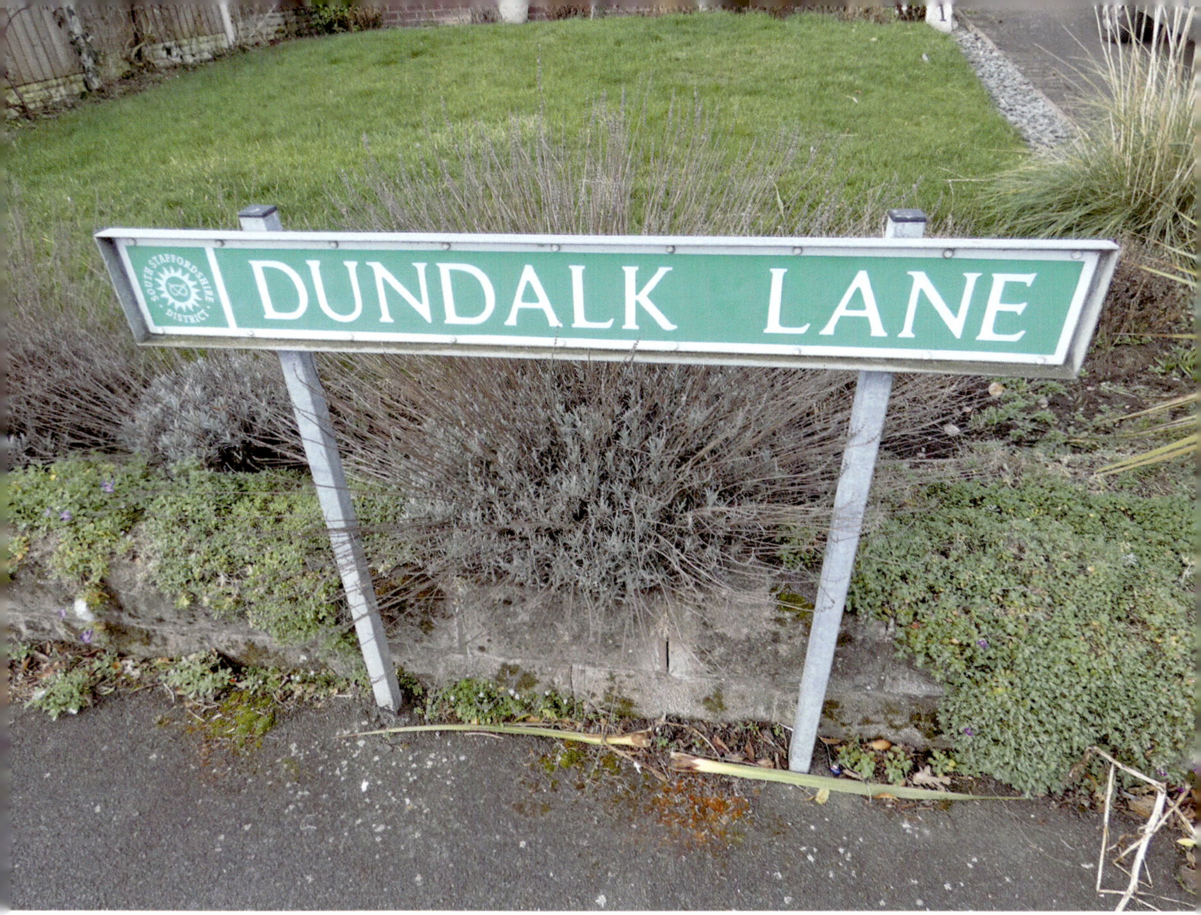

Above and below: Dundalk Lane is a reminder of Dun Duck Lane and the exact location of the Nook Colliery.

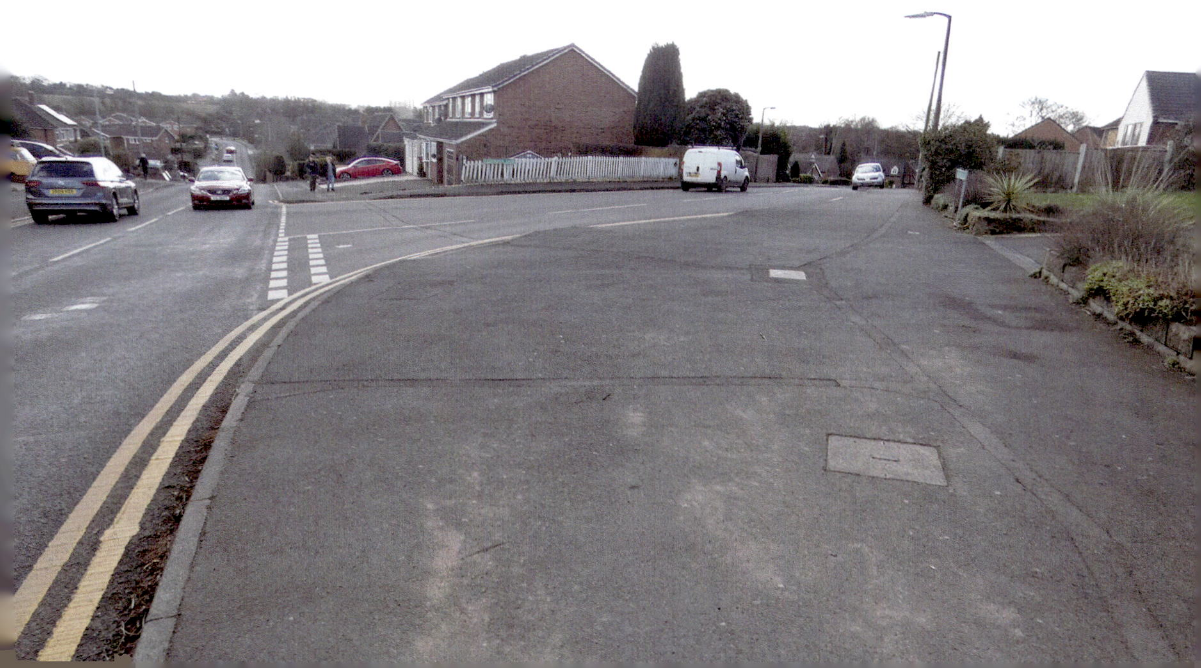

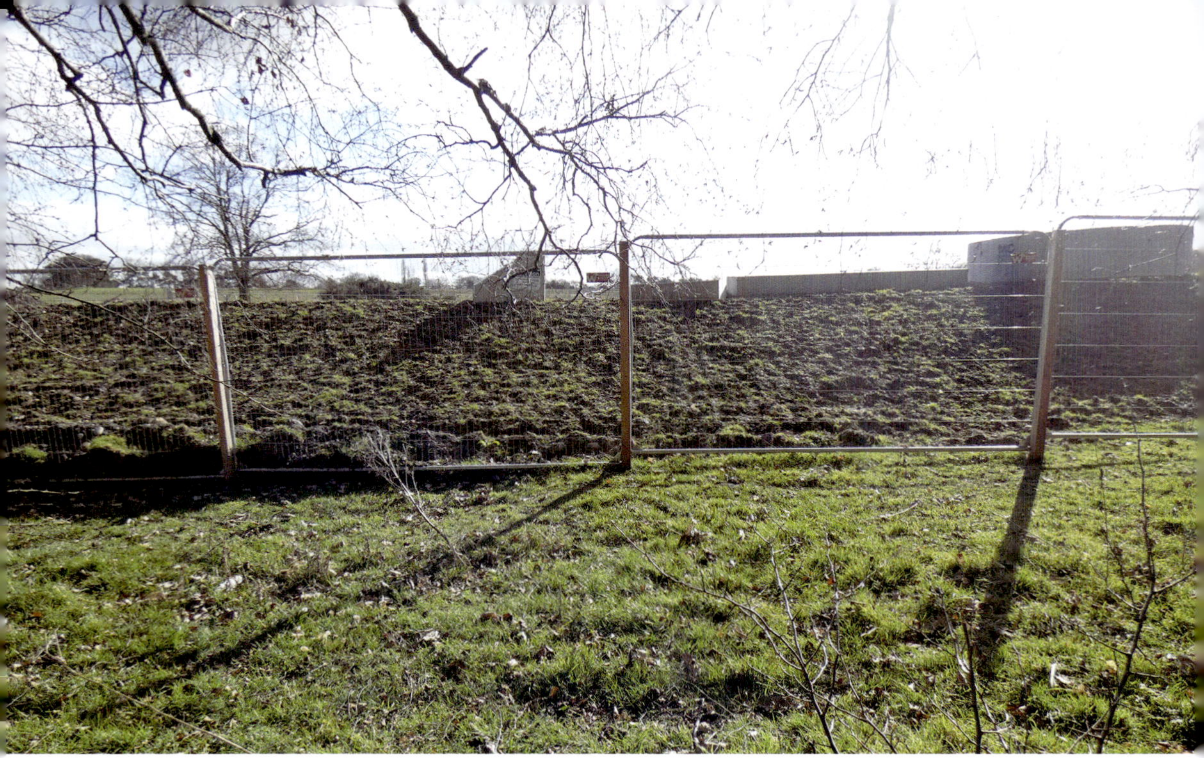

Above: Spring Meadow Colliery once overshadowed this verdant pasture.

Below: Another view of Spring Meadow Colliery.

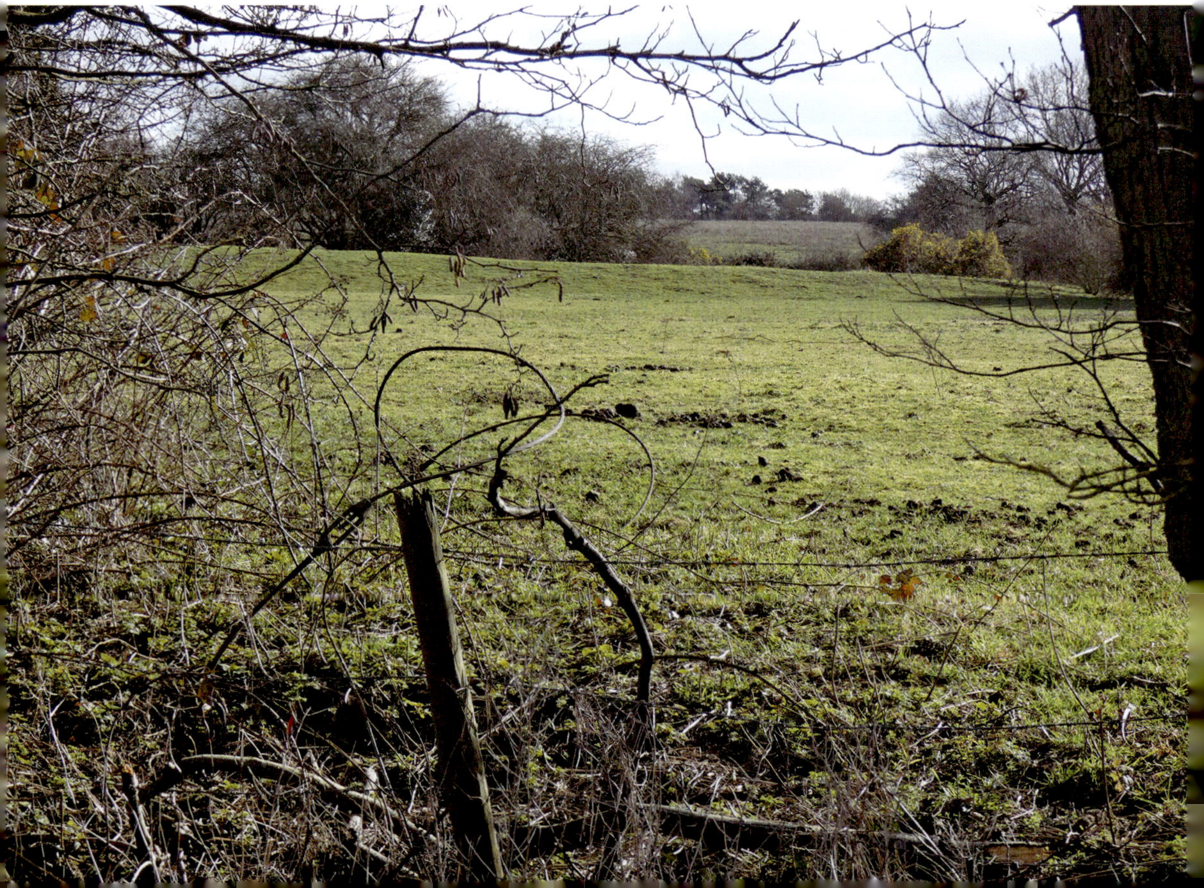

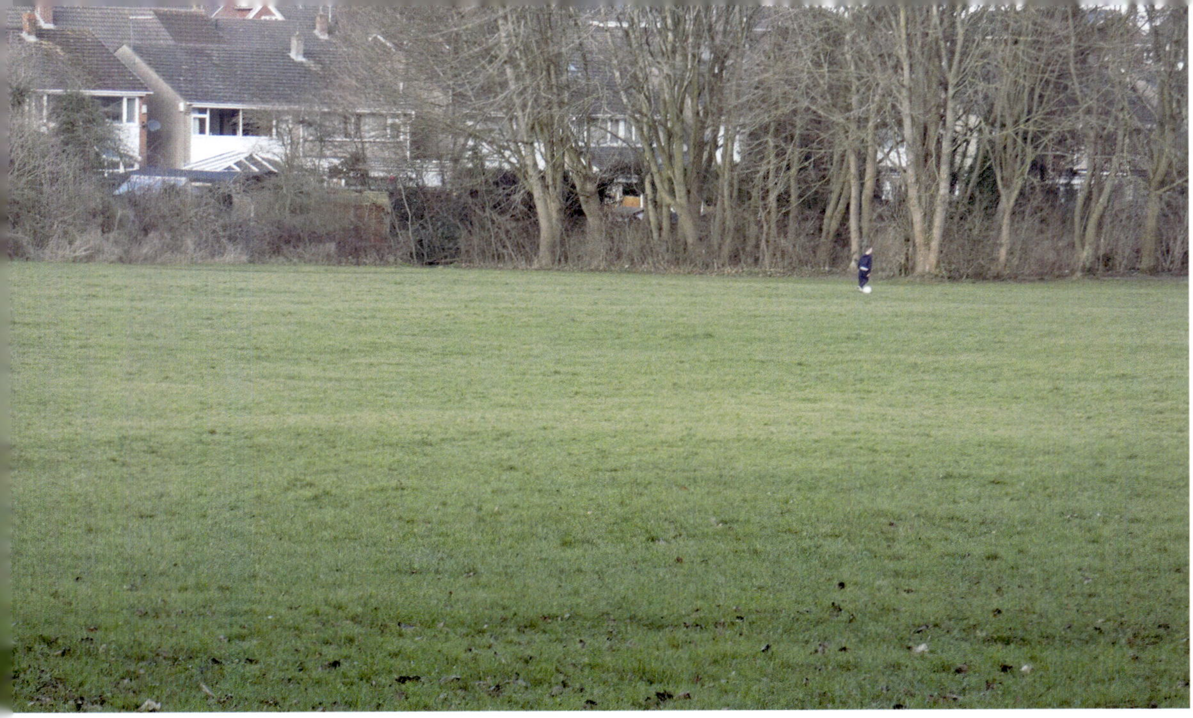

Bulls Meadow Colliery once occupied this area.

The remains of Caddicks Farm Colliery lie beneath the gap between Gorsey Lane and the railway line on what is now the Caddicks Farm housing estate in Lower Landywood. Records are unclear as to when it closed, but no production figures are available after 1952.

Landywood Colliery's remains are hidden to the northwest of Strawberry Lane and between the Wyrley Branch of the Wyrley and Essington Canal and Upper Landywood Lane. Note this lane would be known as Halts Lane until sometime during the 1890s, the colliery remaining in production until 1940.

Hatherton Colliery, officially in Great Wyrley, lay to the west of Streets Lane and 330 yards north of the junction with Upper Landywood Lane. This mine closed in 1876.

The premises of the Wyrley Cannock Colliery Company was, until closure in 1875, based on a site in Landywood adjacent to Landywood Lane and opposite Streets Lane.

Closing in 1969, Yew Tree Drift Mine stood off Old Landywood Lane, where all above ground signs covered an appreciable eight acres, with boundaries formed by the present-day Broad Lane, Long Lane, and New Landywood Lane.

Of the Norton Cannock Collieries the No. 1 colliery stood around 150 yards east of the A34 between Hobble Lane End and Newtown. This was never a working pit, but only a trial sinking. An abattoir later stood on this site. Coal production here came from No. 2 colliery, otherwise known as Fair Oak, located to the northwest of the junction of the A34 and Long Lane, some 710 yards from No. 1 colliery, and where mobile homes were later erected.

Cannock Lodge Colliery, 440 yards west of the A34 at Newtown, had its own basin on the Wyrley Branch of the Wryley and Essington Canal. All the pits here were connected to the railway, specifically the Walsall to Rugeley line which, up to the 1880s, had been known as the Cannock Branch of the South Staffordshire Line. Two shafts, Nos 5 and 6, were about 220 yards west of the Freemasons Arms on the A34. Each shaft had a basin connecting them to the Lord Hays Branch of the Wyrley and Essington Canal, which passed beneath the same A34 trunk road.

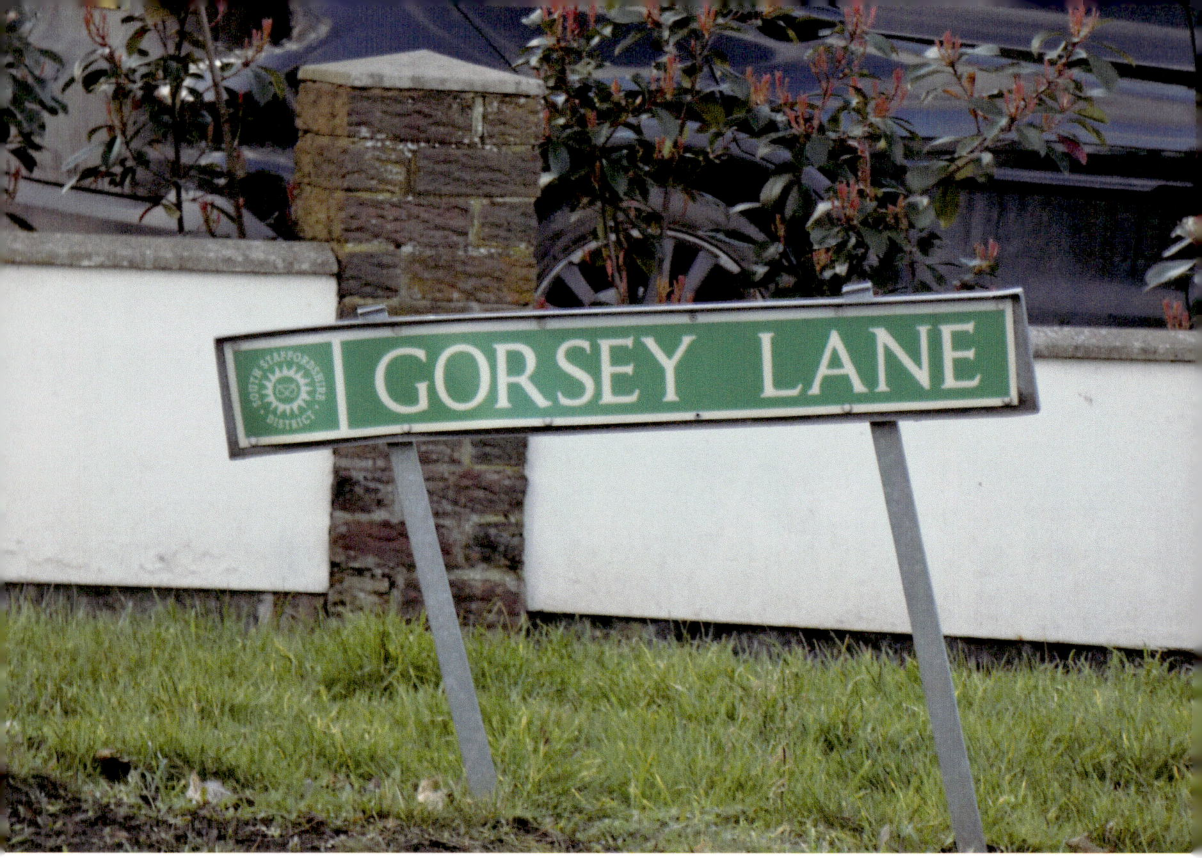

Above: Caddicks Farm Colliery had its home near here.

Below: Today just a signpost points the way to the former Landywood Colliery.

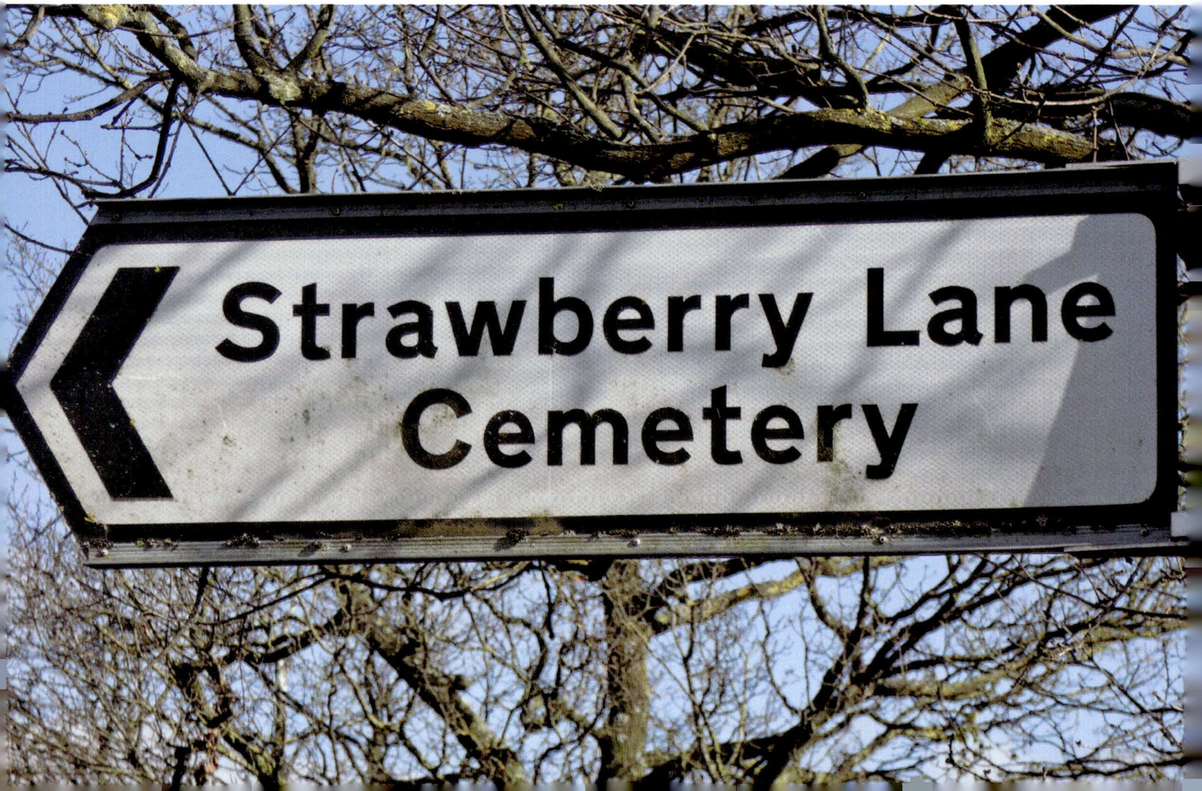

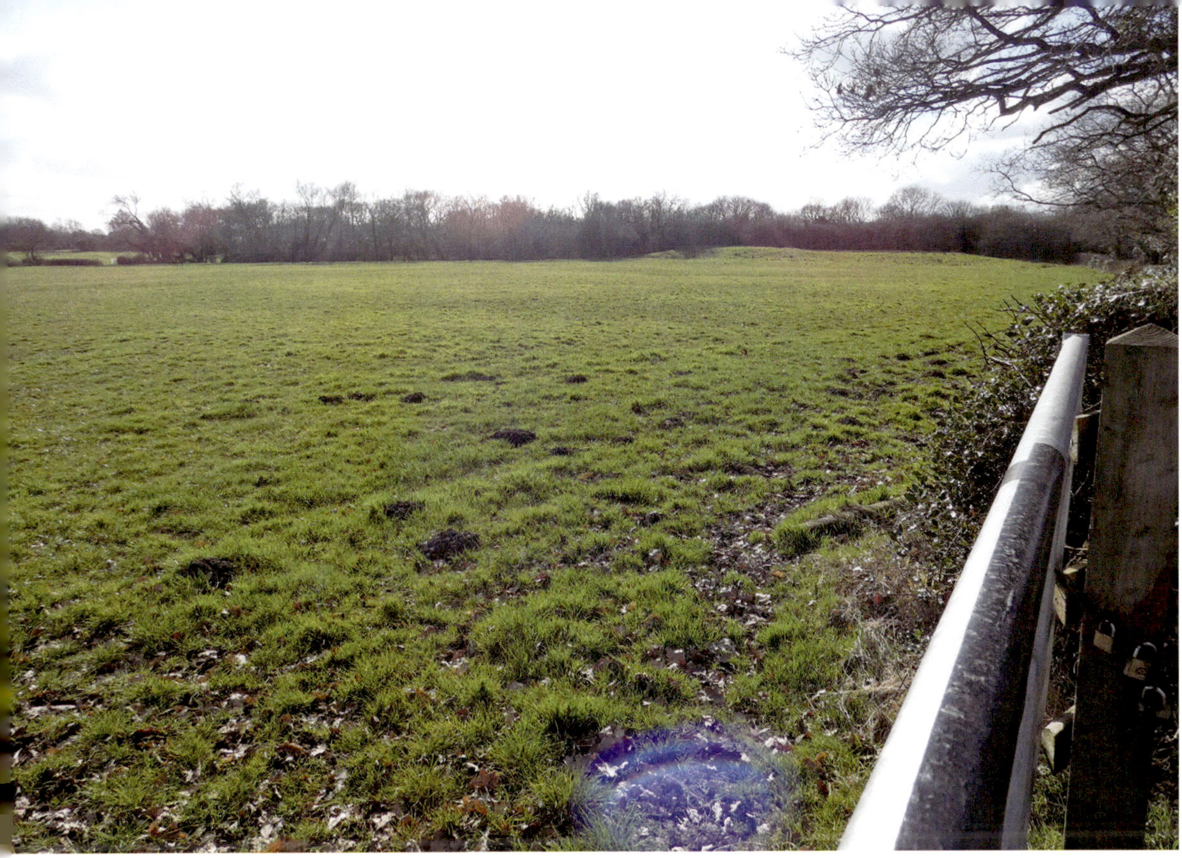

Above: The nearest it is possible to locate Norton Cannock No. 1 Colliery's site…

Below: ….as a housing estate now occupies the site.

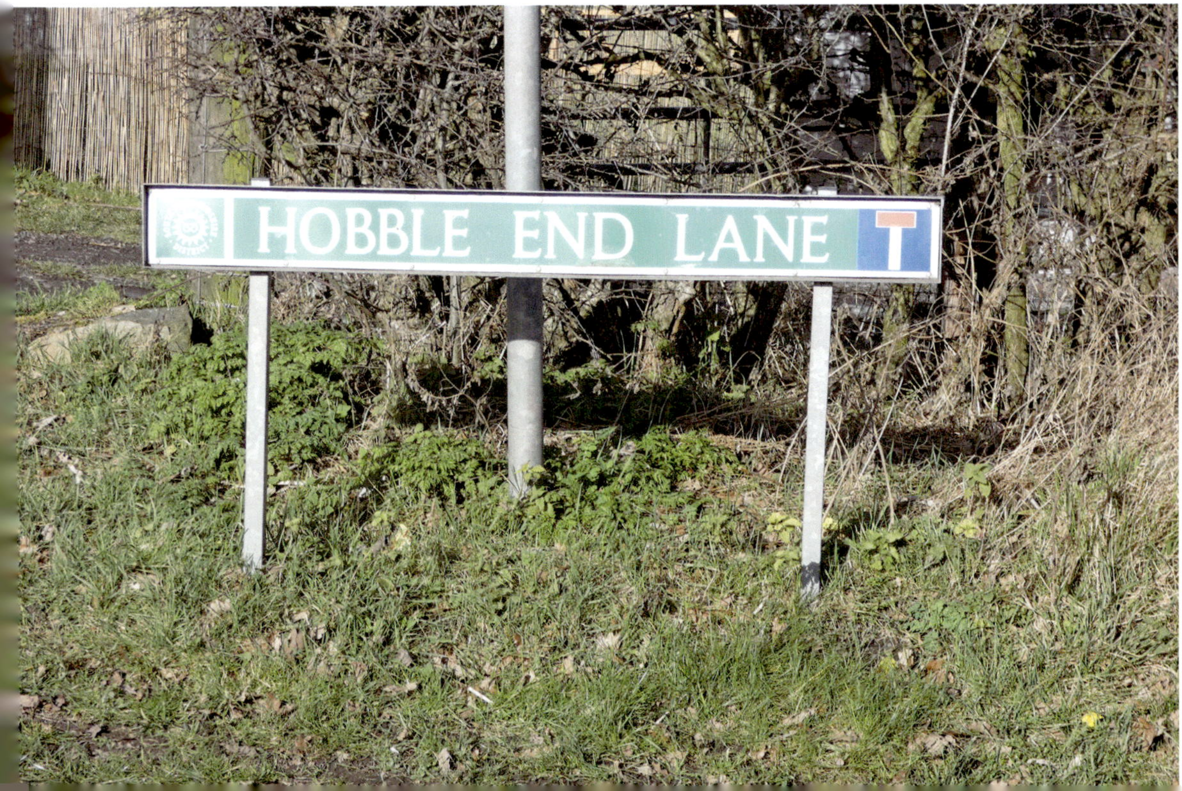

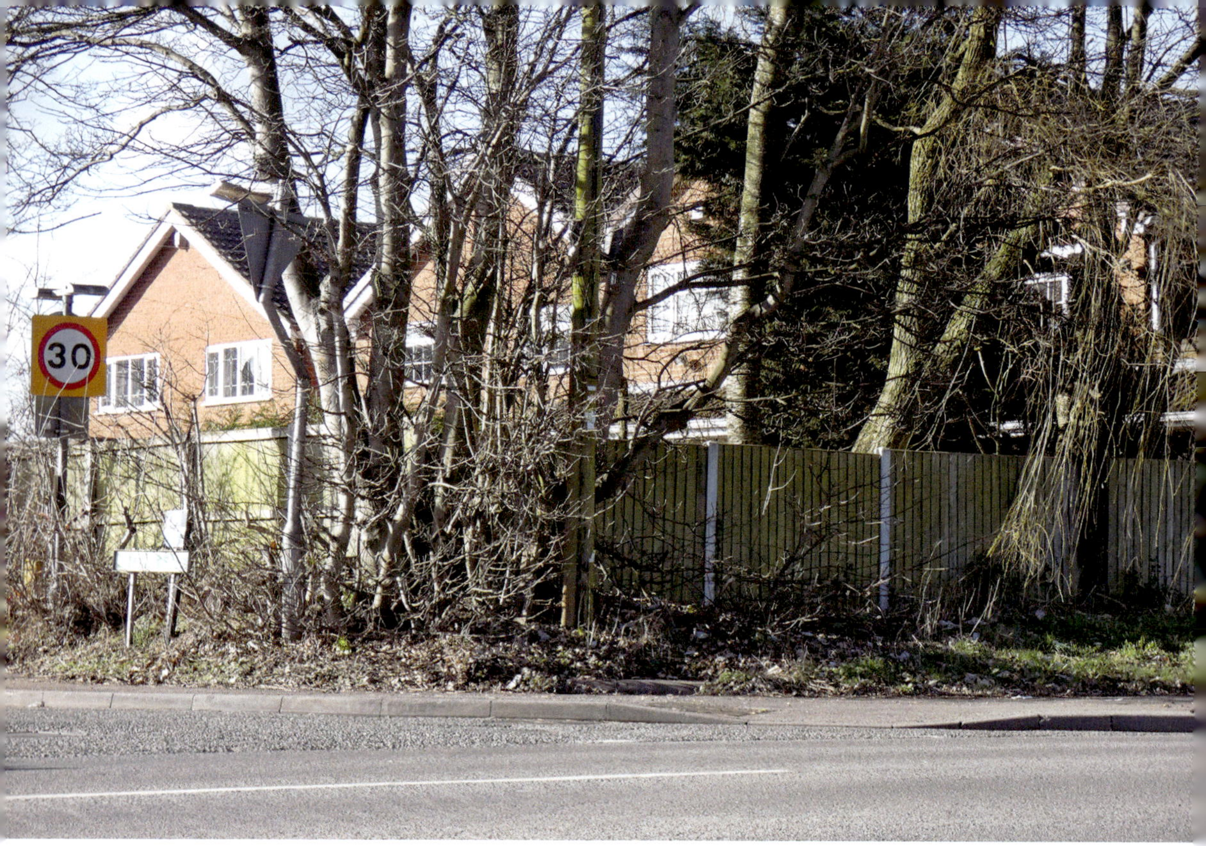

The nearest it is possible to locate Norton Cannock No. 2 Colliery's site and probable location of the former abattoir.

Old Mitre Colliery stood at the end of a western extension of the Wyrley Branch of the Wyrley and Essington Canal, some 220 yards north of where the road crosses the M6, and 300 yards east of Bursnips Road and the Old Mitre public house, from where the colliery took its name.

High Hill Colliery closed around 1840 and stood in Essington to the south of Hobnock Road and east of Brownshaw Lane, later the site of a community centre.

Hilton Colliery, some 220 yards west of Sneyd Farm and 440 yards to the north of Sneyd Lane. Closing in 1901, the site would be recognisable to those who worked here, for the M6 motorway now comes through this site.

The same motorway lies ¼ of a mile to the west of what had been Essington Farm Colliery. Closing in 1904, it was three-quarters of a mile west of where Broad Lane crosses the Walsall to Rugeley railway track.

The nine shafts which were Springhill Colliery closed in 1916. It stood north-west of Bloxwich on land between the Cannock branch of the Wyrley and Essington Canal and the line of the railway between Walsall and Cannock.

Also known as the Struggling Monkey, the Sneyd Colliery near Sneyd Lane in Bloxwich spread both north and south of the lane and west and east of the railway line between Walsall and Rugeley. The mine closed in 1918.

Just 50 yards to the north of Sneyd Lane and between Vernon Way and Broad Lane once stood the Oaks Pit. Today a school is on this site.

In what is now the New Invention area, 660 yards west of Essington Road and 660 yards north of Lichfield Road, stood the Miles Meadow Colliery until closure in 1908.

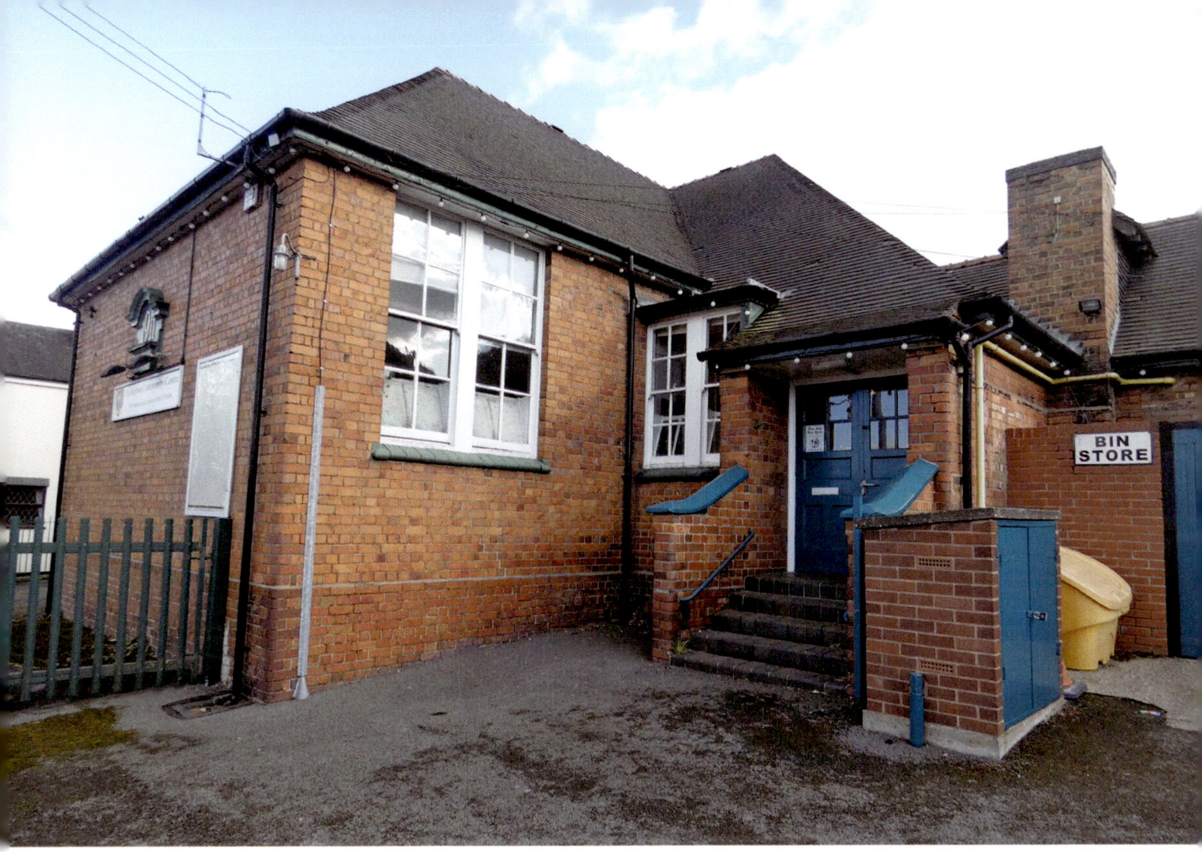

Above: High Hill Colliery is now the site of Essington Community Centre.

Below: Essington Farm Colliery, now given over to a cemetery.

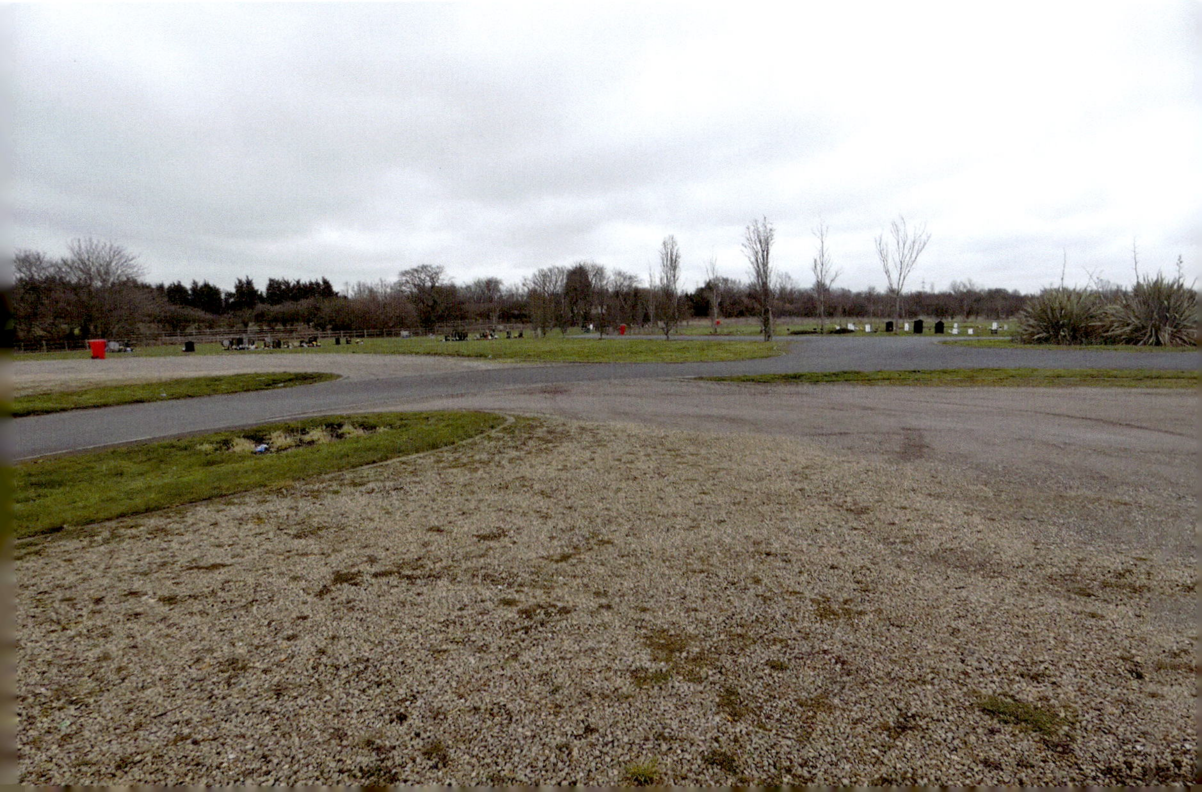

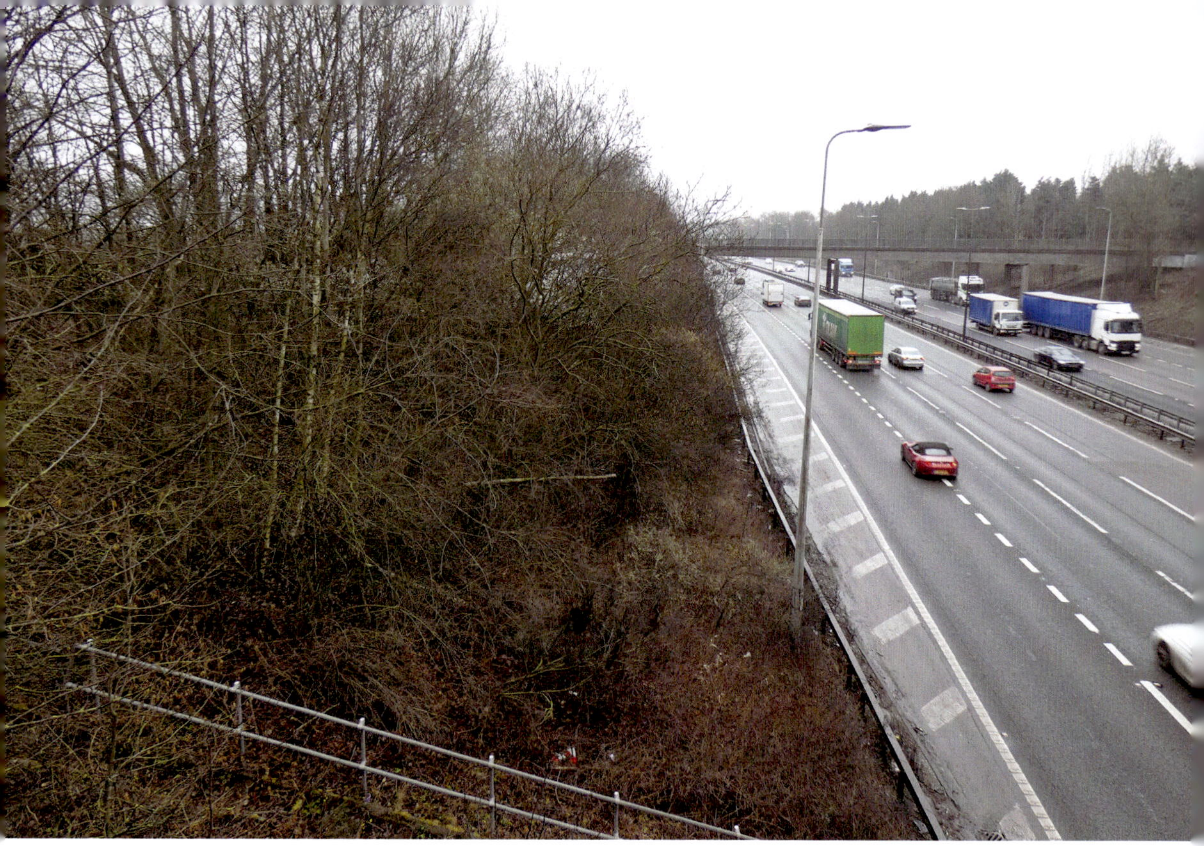

The motorway now crosses the former Essington Farm Colliery.

Wood Farm Colliery closed in 1934. More than forty shafts stood in an area bordered by the Sneyd Reservoir to the north, the Wolverhampton branch of the Wyrley and Essington Canal to the east, Wood Lane to the south, and Pooles Lane to the west – the latter known as Sneyd Lane in the 1880s. As with other former mines above, the M6 motorway runs northwest to southeast right through the area.

Jeavons Pit lay 220 yards south of the Lichfield Road, until it closed in 1914, and is now covered by the motorway.

High Road Colliery lay between Pooles Lane and the M6, bounded to the east by Wood Farm Colliery and to the west Short Heath Colliery, the latter exhausted by the time these shafts had been sunk. High Road Colliery itself closed in 1910.

Station Colliery, named for the nearby Bloxwich Station on the Walsall to Cannock railway line to which it was linked by a tramway, closed in 1896. Its main buildings were alongside the junction of Willenhall Lane with Moreland Road, the property of a Mr Brayford. Bloxwich Station and its sidings were just 150 yards to the north-west of the colliery buildings.

Closing in 1916, the Bloxwich Colliery buildings were between what is now Central Drive and the appropriately named Coalway Road. With Willenhall Lane to the south, a railway line 500 yards to the east, and the Wyrley and Essington Canal 250 yards to the east, the colliery had been well-served by transport links.

Southwest of Bloxwich High Street, in an area bounded by Willenhall Lane, Fryers Road, and Leamore Lane, lay Ward Colliery until closure in the 1870s. Once the Wyrley and Essington Canal ran through this site, with seven shafts on the eastern side and five shafts to the west.

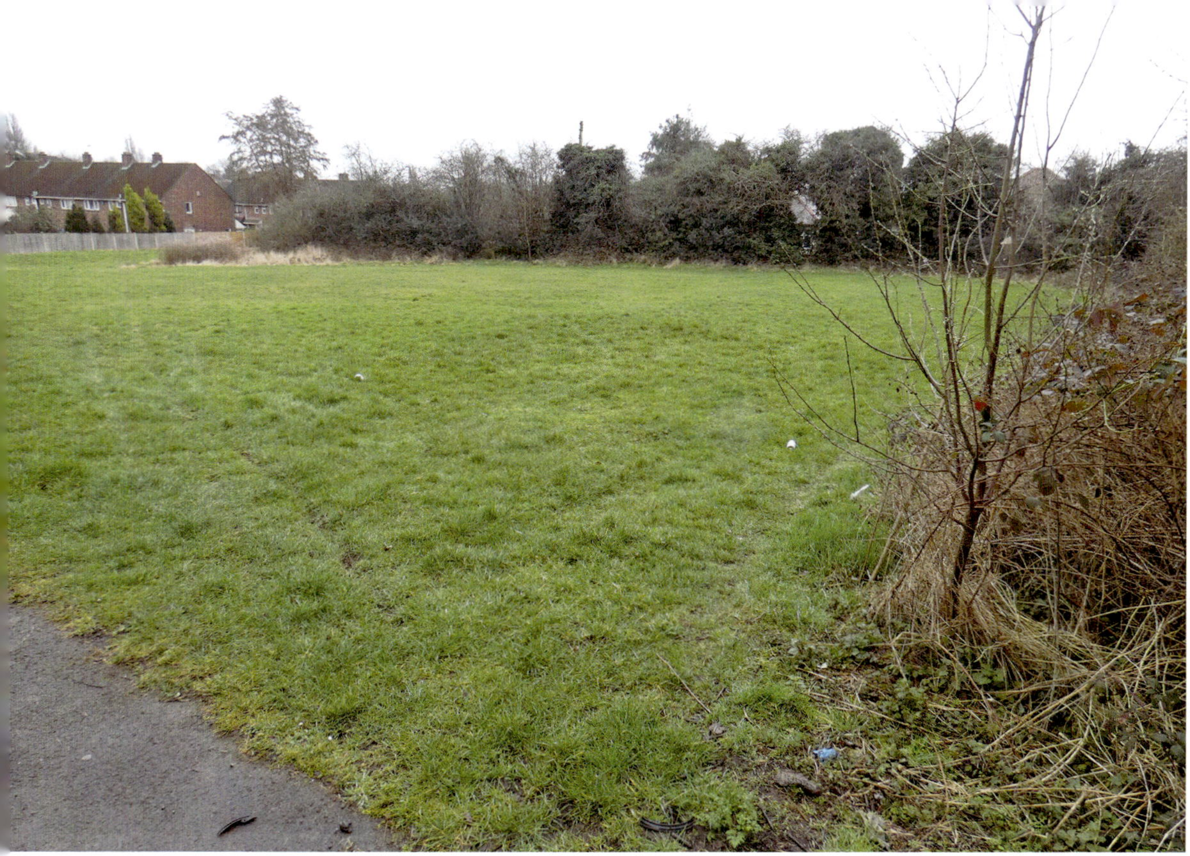

Above: A very different view today from what was once Wood Farm Colliery.

Below: Wood Farm Colliery is now given over to Sneyd Nature Reserve.

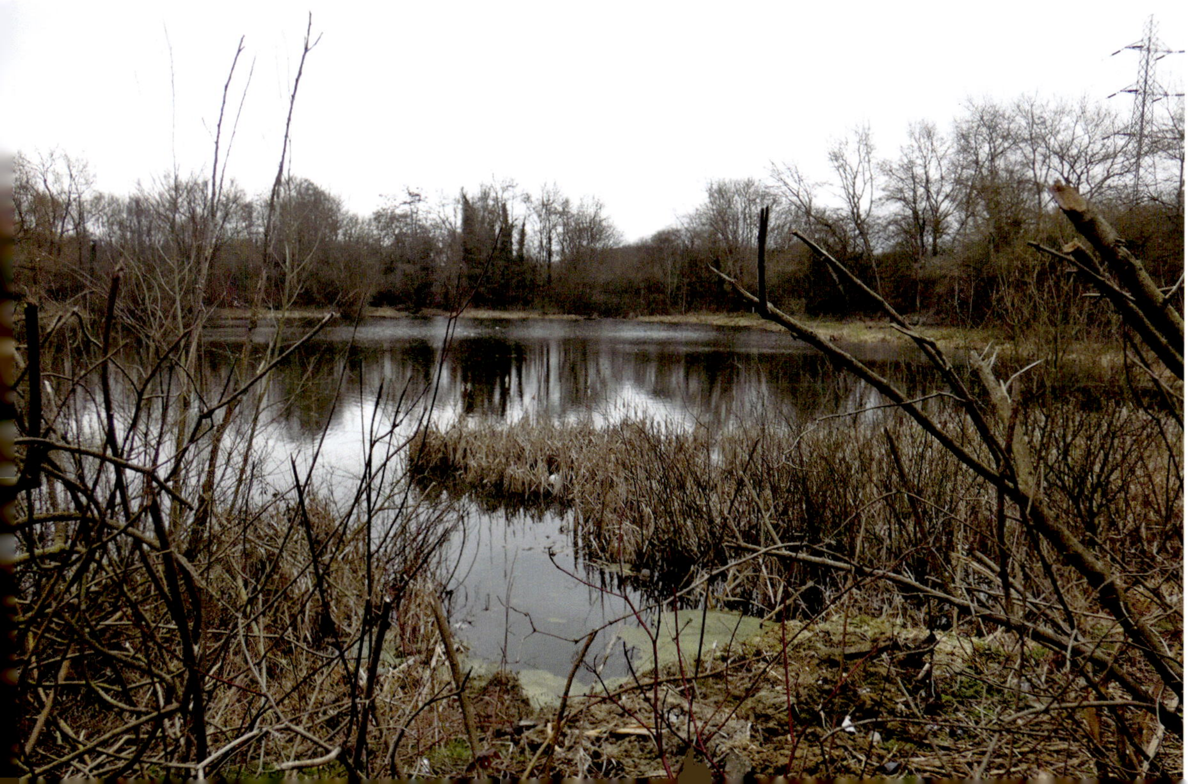

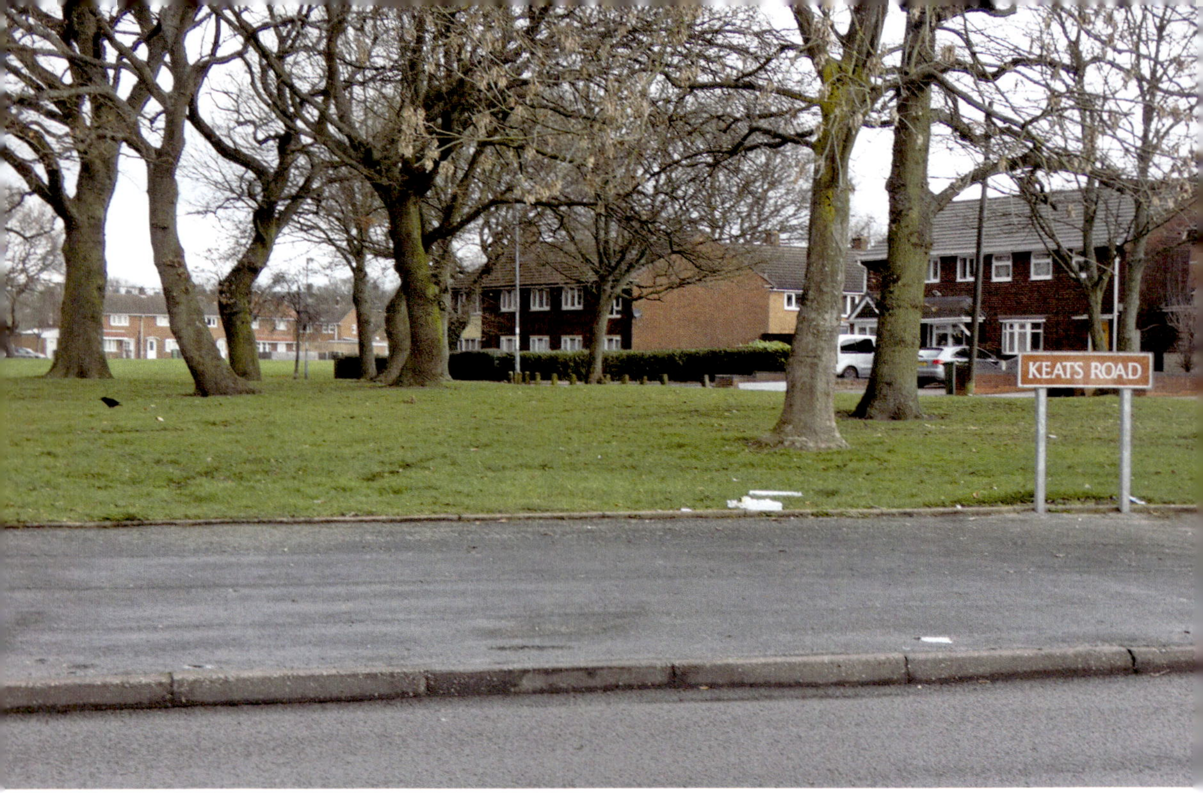

Above: High Road Colliery, now a quiet residential area.

Below: Station Colliery covered this area; it is now residential.

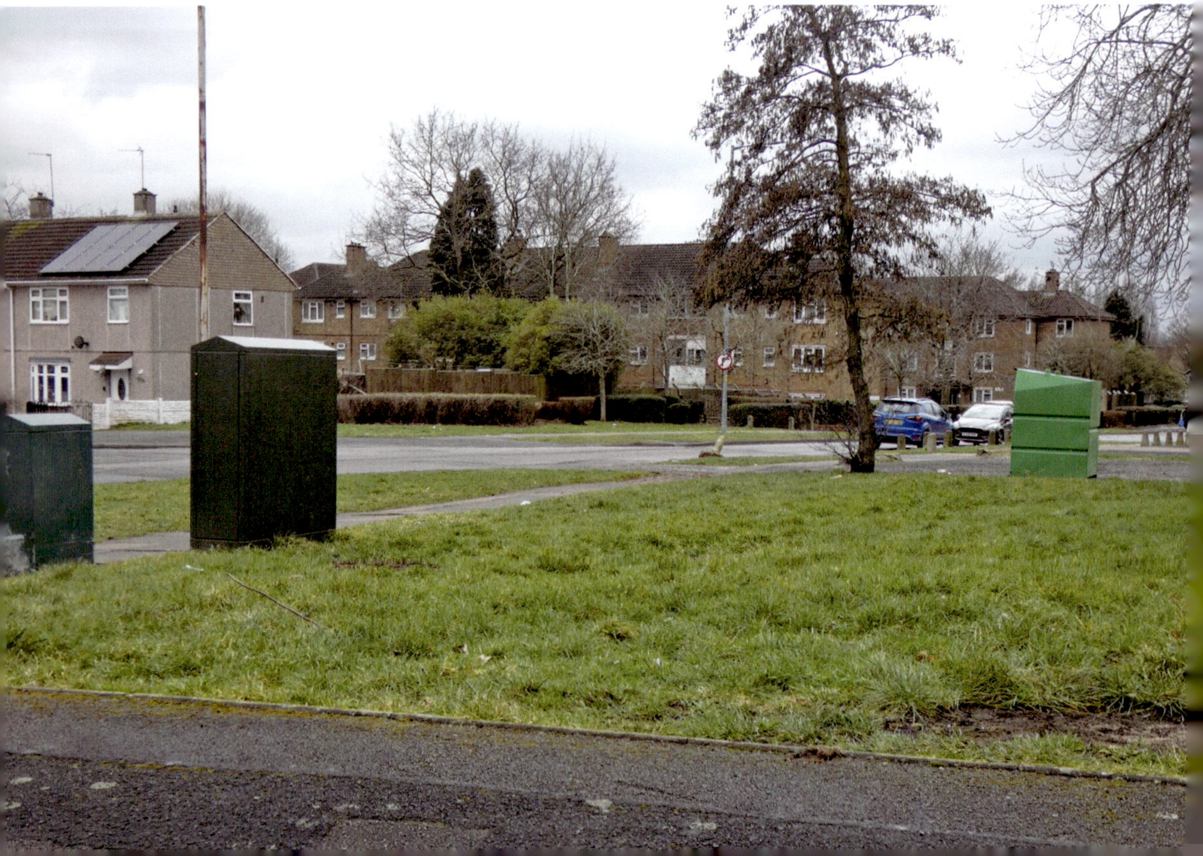

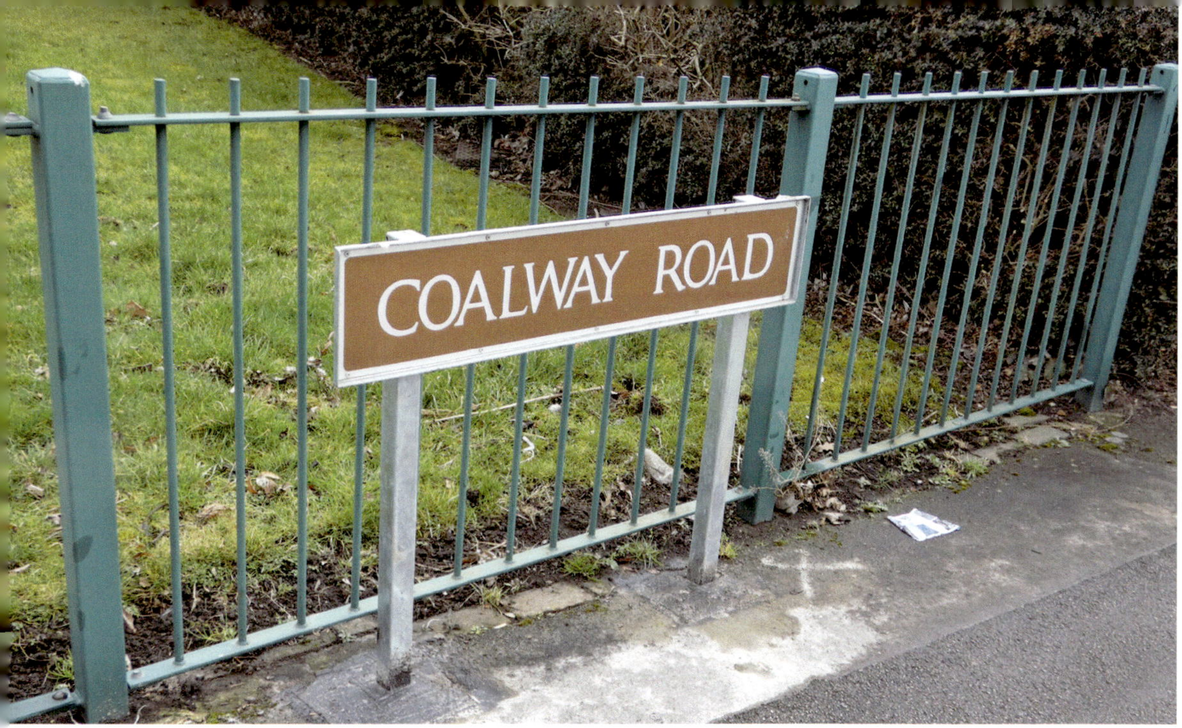

Above: Station Colliery and a reminder of what was once here in the road name.

Below: Ward Colliery relied on the Wyrley and Essington Canal to transport much of its coal.

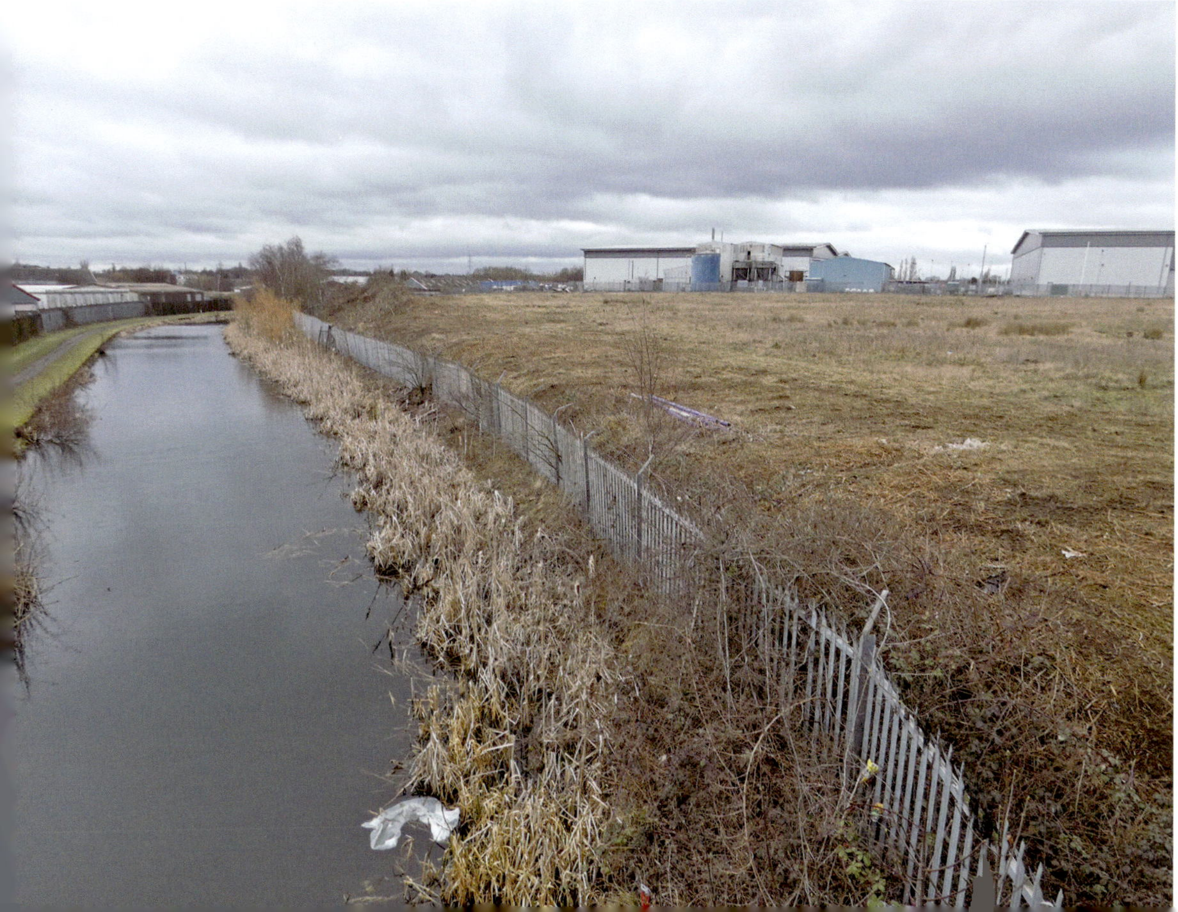

Also known as Coppice Farm Colliery, the Broadway Colliery could be found near what is now the Coppice Sports Centre in New Invention, until closure in 1948. The No. 2 colliery closed the same year, both were found immediately north of the Lichfield Road.

Short Heath Colliery had several shafts, these bordered by Lichfield Road to the north, Pooles Lane to the east, Coltham Road to the south, and Wesley Road in the west.

On the eastern side of the Short Heath Branch of the Wyrley and Essington Canal, and 75 yards to the south of Willenhall Lane, once stood Beechdale Colliery.

Ashmore Park Colliery lay to the north of Ashmore Park and south of the Upper Sneyd Road, at the junction of the Essington Road and Burnsnips Road in New Invention. The colliery drilled numerous shafts in an area approximately one mile from north to south, and three-quarters of a mile from east to west. These pits closed in 1939.

Rounds Coppice Colliery, situated between High Hill and Kitchen Lane in New Invention, boasted four shafts. Shaft Nos 1 and 2 were adjacent to High Hill Road, while 3 and 4 were three hundred yards to the northwest until closure in 1900.

Allens Rough Colliery, closing in 1939, once boasted two shafts and a drift mine located 440 yards south of Sneyd Lane and 150 yards east of Essington Road.

Rough Farm Colliery stood at the junction of Sneyd Lane and Crab Lane until closure in 1930.

Pools Hayes Colliery had its main building to the north of Lichfield Road and west of Essington Road, until it closed in 1948. This part of New Invention is now known as Nightingale Crescent.

Coppice Farm Colliery's former site.

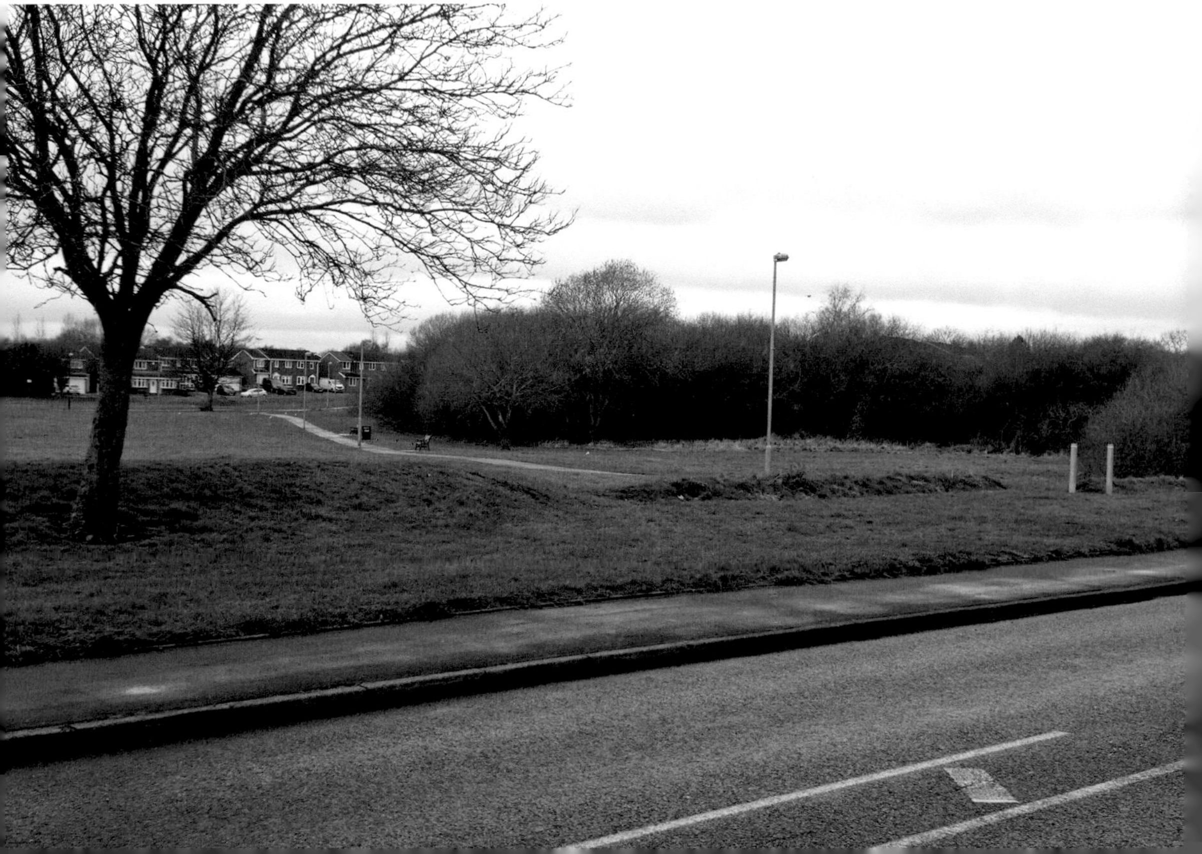

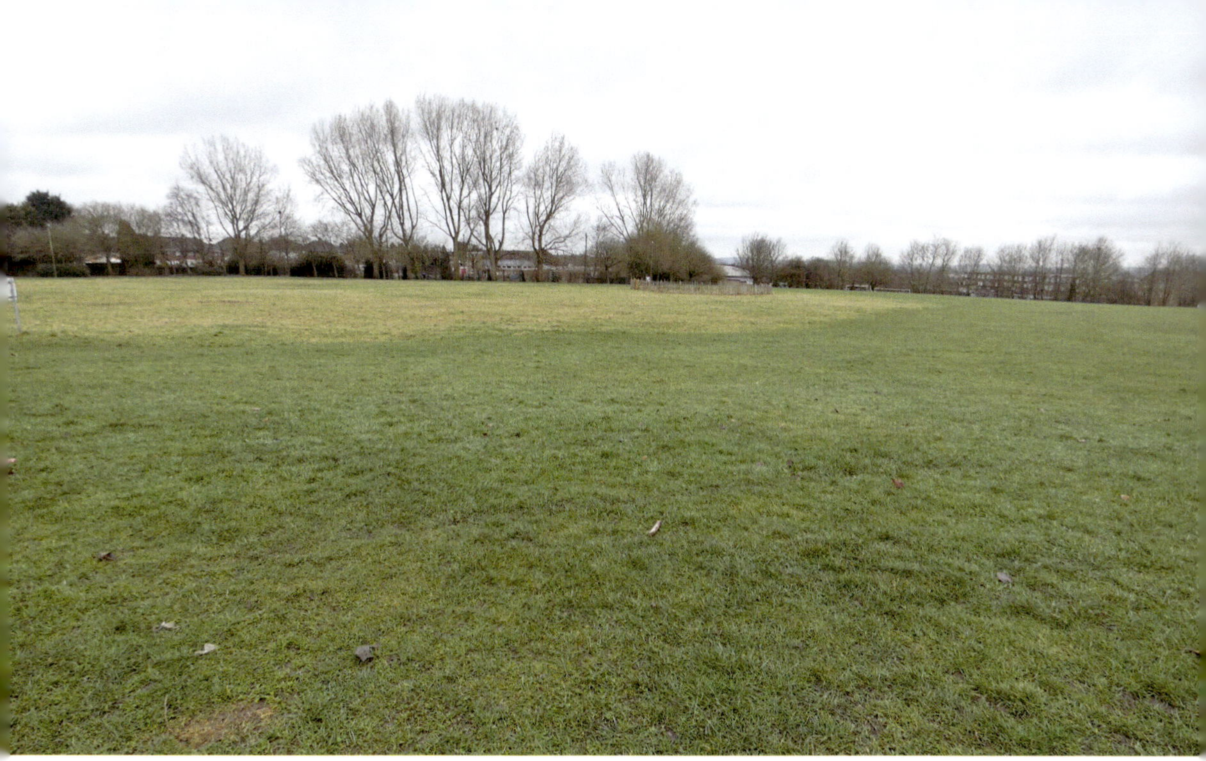

Above: Ashmore Park Colliery site is now a leisure area designated Ashmore Park.

Below: The former site of Rounds Coppice Colliery.

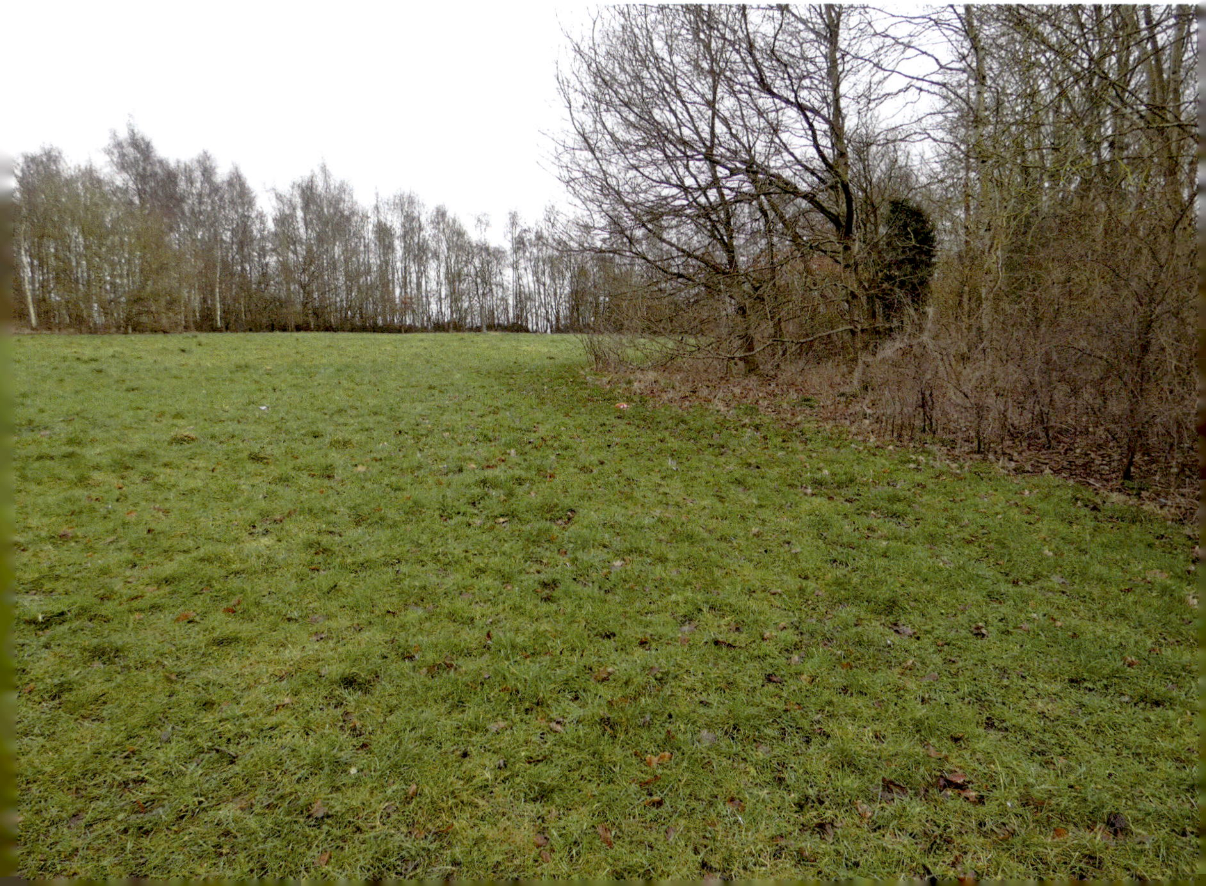

New Invention Colliery closed around 1840. It stood to the west of Essington Road and four hundred yards north of Lichfield Road.

Closing in 1885, Castle Bridge Colliery lies under a spot 22- yards north of Lichfield Road and just to the east of Linthouse Lane.

Perry Hall Colliery closed around 1885. Located in New Invention, it can be found 250 yards south of Lichfield Road and a hundred yards east of Broad Lane North.

Closing in 1894, Coltham Colliery lay west of the junction of High Road and Straight Road at Short Heath.

Newfield Colliery lay in the Leamore area, ¾ of a mile south of Bloxwich Church. The area is marked by the boundaries formed by Bloxwich Road, Leamore Lane, and Green Lane in what was then the 32-acre Newfield Estate.

A steel tube manufacturer once occupied the site formerly occupied by the Green Lane Colliery. Standing on the northern side of the Harden Arm of the Wyrley and Essington Canal, this colliery closed in 1859.

Closing in 1877, the Hatherton Colliery stood near Bloxwich Road between Fryers Road and Reeves Road. The current Irvine Road is the closest landmark to the where the main buildings and shafts once stood.

Harden Colliery lay between Leamore and Harden, half a mile east of Bloxwich Road and adjacent to what is now Harden Road and Harden Close.

Castle Bridge Colliery, east of Linthouse Lane.

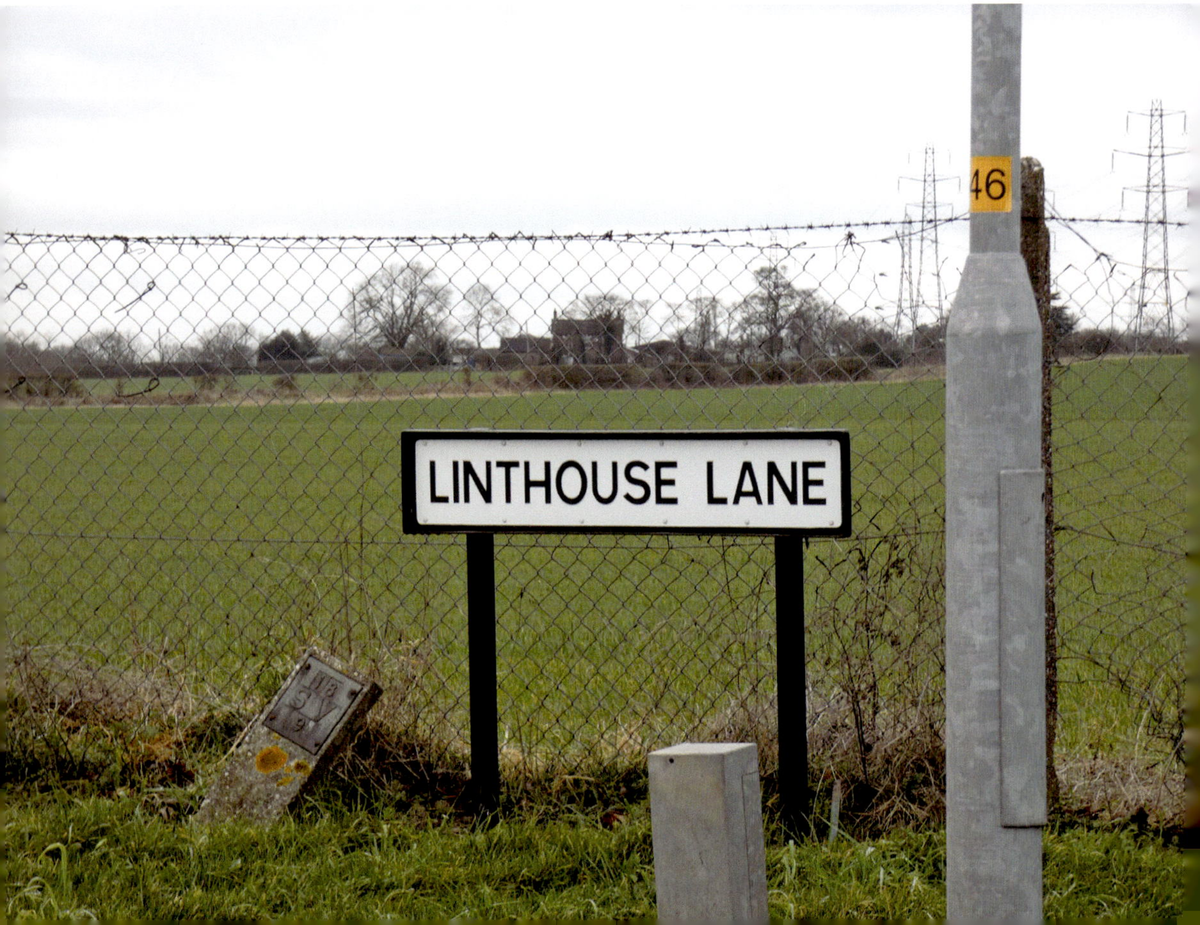

Forest Colliery, south of Leamore and 150 yards east of Bloxwich Road. It was later occupied by the Forest Comprehensive School. Elm Road and Hawbush Road were on the western boundary.

Bentley Colliery closed in 1903. It was situated 100 yards southeast of the Short Heath Branch of the Wyrley and Essington Canal where it stretched under Bentley Lane. Close to Bentley Station and with a municipal golf course acting as its western boundary, today the site is partly buried by the M6 motorway.

Bentley Park Colliery occupied an area with borders running from Straight Road to what would become Church Road, and north from Bentley Lane to near the bend in the Short Heath Branch of the Wryley and Essington Canal. These workings closed in 1949.

Bentley Hay Colliery closed around 1850. It occupied a region 250 yards south-west of the Short Heath Branch of the Wyrley and Essington Canal, and north of Bentley Lane which became a part of the municipal golf course.

Bentley Farm Colliery, which shut its doors for the last time in 1923, lay 650 yards west of Green Lane. This had been a part of Reedswood Park and where Stephenson Avenue can now be found.

Roughwood Colliery, closing in 1911, sat on a public open space known as Rough Wood. On the modern map it is bordered to the north by Wood Lane and the M6 motorway to the east.

Derelict coal mine with pitheads on Yew Tree Hills, facing south with Client Hills on the horizon. (Ref: pst/4257, courtesy of Dudley Archives and Local History Service)

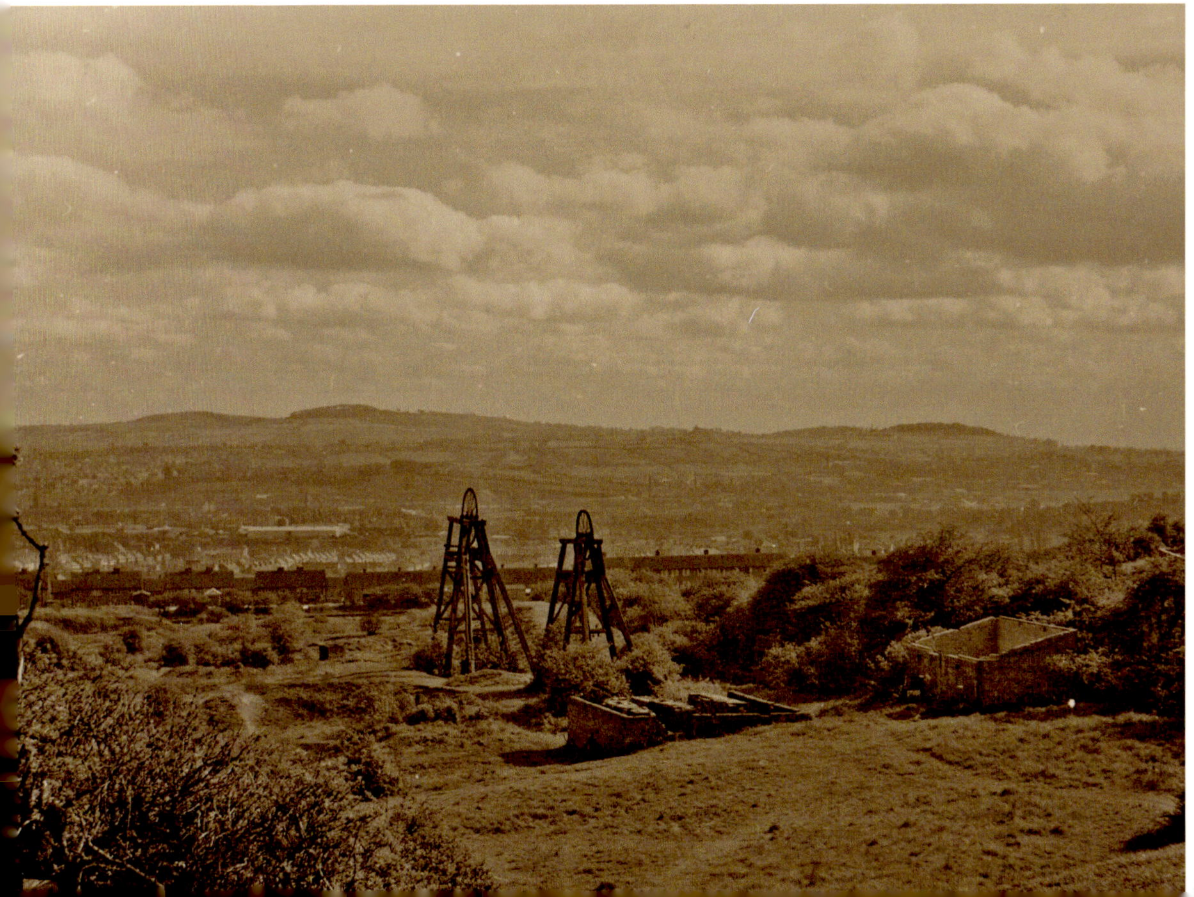

19

BROWNHILLS COMMON COAL WORKINGS

Here we are moving across towards the area around Brownhills Common. Up until 1841 these collieries had only worked those seams named the Deep Seam and the Shallow Seam. Through faulting and folding, these coal seams lay at a gradient of 1 in 13, running out to the north-west and with the shallowest end in the Pelsall Road area. It is an indication of how shallow this seam is that it can be seen in it outcropping in the cellars of the Swan Tavern in Pelsall Road.

Watling Street Colliery, unsurprisingly found on the A5, to the south side of that Roman road and east of the Walsall Wood extension of the Midland Railway, closed in 1903.

Kingswood Colliery closed in the 1960s. The only surviving landmark which can be used to locate this part of the Brownhills Coppice Colliery is the Rising Sun public house, with Kingswood about 250 yards to the rear of a building which is very much in danger of disappearing after recent fire damage.

Similarly, the Rising Sun Colliery, this closing in 1960, lay south of Chester Road and 350 metres east of the public house which gave it a name.

Brereton Collieries may be closed for coal production, but evidence remained into the twenty-first century. At the end of the nineteenth century a tunnel constructed under the main road permitted the loads hauled by rope to be extended the entire length from the levels as far as the canal basin. Known as the Ginnes Line, it covered more than a thousand yards and dropped comparatively steeply by 160 feet to the canal side. Closure of the mine did not put an end to the life of the tunnel, for during the Second World War it served as an air-raid shelter, then became an underpass, and not until 2003 was it sealed off and filled with concrete.

The Old Engine Colliery closed in 1950, extraction of coal from this shaft added nothing to that extracted from neighbouring pits and, rather than working two or three pits, the decision was made to close it. Earlier the same was true of the Belfast Pit, a smaller mining concern, had already closed by 1903.

Closing in 1908, the Coppice Colliery was also known as the Coppy or Big Pit. Flaxley Green Shaft was the last operating here, although it had only been sunk as a trail shaft for the Hayes and Hall pits around 1850. In the first year of the twentieth century the shaft had been widened to around ten feet and the depth greatly increased down to 508 feet, although that depth was never used to extract coal or anything else as it had never been equipped with pumps at the time of the disaster on 15 February 1908. Flooding of the mine, killing three men, saw an immediate closure of the Coppice Colliery. Its shafts were left open to monitor water levels, but by July 1909 the workings were completely submerged, and water had risen to within 84 feet of the surface. Those three men trapped underground and who drowned that day were never recovered.

Hill Pit's buildings stood on the high ground behind the Holly Bush Inn, this later known as Dinah's Knob for Dinah Hawley lived in the converted buildings at the end of the nineteenth century, the pit closing in 1850.

In November 1828 one Joseph Palmer was granted a lease for the Hayes Colliery, then valued at £4,213. On his death in 1837, the mine passed to his widow Sarah Palmer, but the lease ended ten years later owing to poor management. ownership passing back to the Marquis of Anglesey. Joseph and Sarah Palmer may not be well remembered themselves, but their son William certainly achieved notoriety – he most often referred to as the Rugeley Poisoner. The Brick Kiln Colliery had undergone a change of name and was known as Brereton Colliery when it closed in 1872. Startley Shafts closed in the 1870s.

20

BRERETON COLLIERIES

Again, here we will look at the collieries which have left their mark below ground. This time we turn to Brereton and highlight those whose locations are largely known. The Flaxley Drift closed in 1959, one of the last workings to cease production, doing so some fifteen months before the final Brereton Colliery shut its doors. Unusually, we know there are no equipment remains below ground here, for everything had been extracted and sold at auction – this included the ropes. A series of dams designed to contain any explosions were constructed, these also sealing off the workings for eternity.

Cannock Old Coppice Colliery closed in 1900, by which time it had become known as the Hawkins Colliery. Lying immediately south of the junction of Lodge Lane and Coppice Lane in Cheslyn Hay, this area later set aside as an industrial estate bordering the M6 motorway. Hammerwich Colliery, the No. 1 pit, was located adjacent to the Anglesey canal extension until it closed in 1857. Uxbridge Colliery, the No. 2 pit, also known as the Fly, closed in 1940. Today the site is marked by the end of Church Street in Chasetown, better seen as the site of the Burntwood Rugby Club. A plaque giving details of the former use of this site has been erected in the rugby club's main office building.

Brereton's No. 4 Colliery once stood at the end of Union Street, Chasetown, until closure in 1877.

The Plant, more often known as No. 3 Colliery, closed in 1959 and could be found south-west of the end of Plant Lane opposite Ironstone Road, an industrial estate off Miners Way. Part of the Burntwood Ring Road also give clues to what lies beneath the ground here.

Brereton's No. 5 Colliery, having closed in 1920, could be found opposite Princess Street in Chase Terrace on the Cannock Road. Cannel Mount, officially No. 6 Colliery, is to be seen when travelling from Five Ways at Heath Hayes and on the right-hand side when descending into Wimblebury, albeit hidden behind trees. Brereton No. 7 Colliery was adjacent to Seven's Road in Prospect Village. It closed in 1961.

Brereton No. 8 Colliery stood closer to Cannel Mount than any other pit, closing in 1962. Hednesford Colliery, also given as Nos 9 and 10 collieries, closed in 1962.

Stubbes Green Colliery is certainly a much better name than Copy Hall Colliery, not least because it helps us to locate the former workings off Stubbes Green Road alongside an arm of the canal cut specially to transport the coal extracted. Shafts remained open until 1930, when a shaft collapse resulted in a large conical crater. Filled with red ash from the tip, it remained untouched until 1977, when some 30 feet of this fill were removed to expose the shafts once more and prepare the ground for capping appropriate for the current regulations. Capped, drilled and grouter by a contractor, vents were provided to the atmosphere as demanded by the Effluent Disposal Scheme. These shafts are best found by locating the Salvesen Brickworks in Stubbes Green Road, Aldridge where the shafts lie behind those works.

Speedwell Colliery, also known as Victoria Colliery, stood near Aldridge Station until closing in 1881. Closing in December 1930, the Leighswood Colliery, alternatively recorded as both Aldridge No. 2 or Dry Bones Pit, lay between Brickyards Lane and Walsall Wood branch railway line. Unbelievably, the shaft remained open to the sky for more than two decades, with only a wall erected to prevent any interested parties from falling in. Spoil and red ash helped to fill the shaft in the late 1950s, the National Coal Board later upgrading the cap to comply with regulations. Today the shaft lies in part under a warehouse in Brickyard Road, Aldridge, that warehouse constructed prior to the updated fill by drilling and grouting the fill. Walsall Wood Colliery closed in 1964.

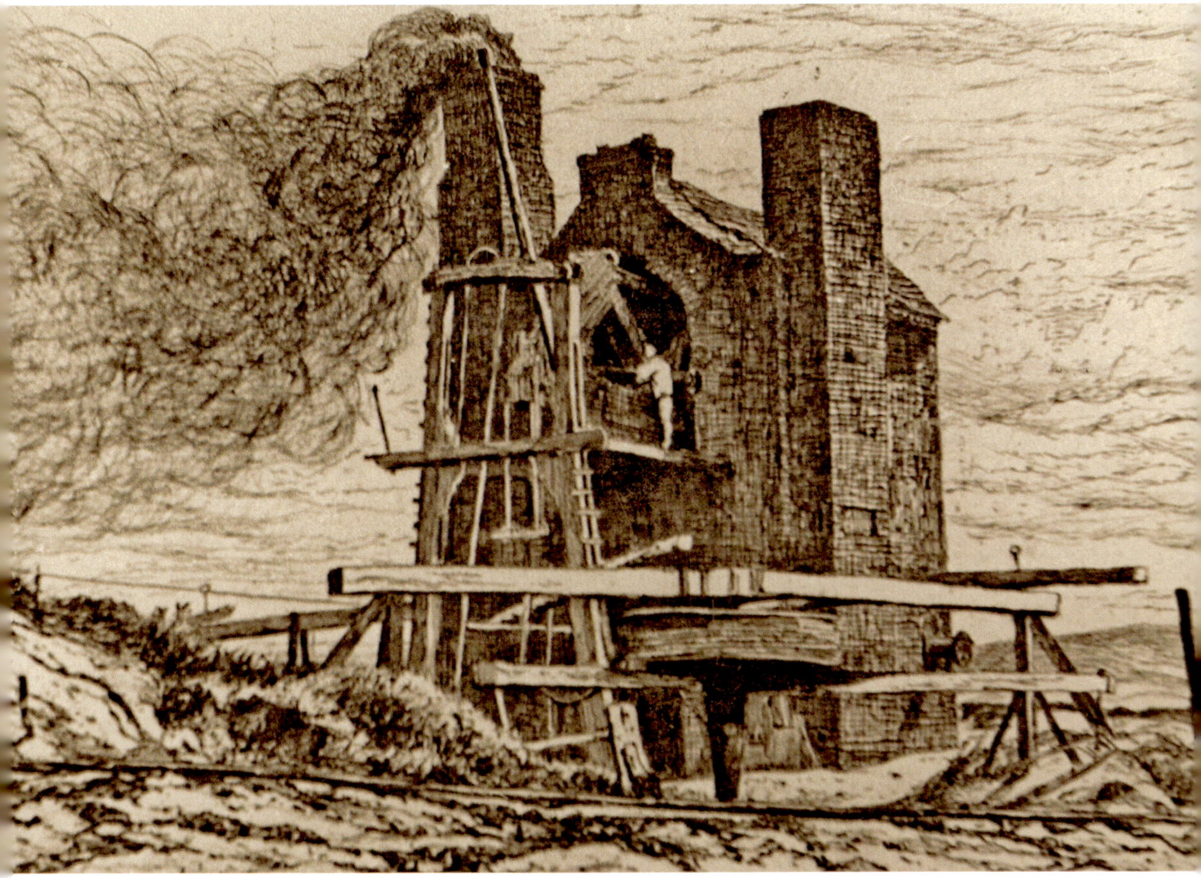

Photograph of an 1872 etching by artist Richard S. Chattock of the working Buffery pit pump. The image shows a crude wooden pit frame and horse gin. The pump would probably have been used to pump out water that was constantly filling the mine shafts. The wooden engine beam can be seen at the top of the engine house. (The original etching was Plate XII from a set of sixteen etchings by the artist on India paper of the coal and iron district of South Staffordshire; Ref: p/1871, courtesy of Dudley Archives and Local History Service)

21

BROWNSHILL COLLIERY

Brownhills Colliery, which is also recorded as the Cathedral Pit, lay some 200 yards south of Watling Street and 600 yards west of the Rising Sun public house at the junction of Watling Street with Chester Road. This pit closed in 1910. Wyrley Common Pit stood on Wyrley Common at the end of Engine Lane in Brownhills until it closed in 1862. Slough Colliery, closing in 1914, could once be found south of Engine Lane/Coppice Lane and about 375 yards south of Pelsall Road.

Yew Tree Colliery stood on the south side of Pelsall Road and just south-east of the aforementioned Slough Colliery. Despite closing in 1856, the remains of the spoil heaps are still readily seen.

Highbridge Colliery had its own basin on the Gilpins Arm of the Wyrley and Essington Canal some 350 yards south of the colliery which stood south of the Pelsall Road.

Wyrley Grove Colliery and Wyrley Grove Colliery No. 3, the latter also recorded as Harrison's or even the Sinking, stood alongside Hazel Lane and had been since that was known as Slacky Lane. Closing in 1967 it is bordered by the A34 and A5 trunk roads. Known as the Mid, the Mid Cannock Colliery closed in 1880. A little over a thousand yards south of Cannock town centre at Rumer Mill, bordered to the north and east by George Street, with the western boundary provided by the Rugeley to Walsall railway, and to the south stood open fields and the Roman road of Watling Street.

Norton Green Colliery, or Conduit No. 4, stood at the junction of Walsall Road and Norton Green Lane, just to the north of Watling Street. The chimney of the original colliery still stands. Closing in 1897 the Conduit No. 1 Colliery could be found on the southerly side of Watling Street on Wyrley Common, where a small industrial estate now stands. This site has been home to, among others, a cycle shop, and a distributor of garden tools.

Conduit Colliery No. 2, closing in 1961, was slightly west of Wilkin Road near where it joins Hednesford Road. Pool Lane Colliery closed in 1961 and the site later developed as a trotting track. This can be found 400 yards north of Watling Street and 50 yards east of Pool Lane. Conduit Colliery No. 3, sometimes referred to as Jerome's, stood ¾ of a mile north of the A5 alongside the Walsall Road and almost in the centre of Norton Canes. Jerome Road runs through here, a reminder of the pit closing in 1949.

Conduit Colliery No. 4, also known as the Norton Green Colliery, closed in 1933 when it stood at the junction of Norton Green Lane and Walsall Road where the original chimney still marks the spot.

Essington Wood Colliery closed in 1889 and Holly Bank Colliery closed in 1895. Allen's Rough Colliery, Sneyd Colliery, Hilton Main Colliery, Cannock and Rugeley Colliery Company closed around the same time, although records are unclear.

Valley Colliery, also known as the Pool Pits, was just east of Hednesford in the valley behind Cockpit Hill on the Hednesford Hills until closing in 1962. Wimblebury Colliery, closing in 1962, could once be found in the valley between Littleworth Road and the village of Wimblebury.

West Cannock Colliery Company closed in 1982. East Cannock Colliery Company closed in 1957, Fair Oak Colliery Company in 1884, and The Fair Lady closed in 1964.

22

PELSALL HALL COLLIERY

Thursday 14 November 1872 is among the most memorable dates for the Cannock Chase Coalfield. For the Pelsall Hall Colliery, this marked the date water flooded the mine to a depth of 35 feet up the main shaft. It took until the following Monday to pump out the water and clear the gas, but this only revealed the roadway to the face to be blocked with debris. This impromptu barrier may be seen as the saving grace for those trapped behind it, keeping the water at bay, but even if that had been the case then it also acted as a barrier to the pumps bringing fresh air into the workings. Hence the sight of the debris told the rescue workers they were not going to find anyone alive behind the debris.

With the fresh air also a problem for rescuers, work to recover the bodies proceeded slowly. Eventually eighteen of the missing men were found at a much higher level, all fully clothed and showing no signs of having been underwater. As the rescuers had thought, cause of death proved to be asphyxiation, not drowning. Another body was found in No. 3 shaft, and a further in the stables with his back broken, where it seems the flood had thrown him onto a board between two stalls. Lastly, they found Michael Cash, his body covered by an upturned tub, a bruise to the cranium showing the force with which he had been thrown against a beam. Clearly, he had not died instantly, for he had one arm wrapped around a prop and the other entangled in a horse's reins. Mr Cash had been the first to notice the water flowing into the workings, and much stronger than previously. He alerted fellow miner Harry Astbury, who told him not to continue working that face but, it seems, he ignored the advice and within fifteen minutes the noise of the water rushing into the workings alerted the other miners to the problem.

It later transpired the water came from old workings, these unrecorded and thus the water levels not monitored. As the new workings were undermining the old, when the two became connected water naturally found its own level. After the mining area had been drained an inspection of the older workings showed, through examining the methods and supports used, they were very much older than those of the latter half of the nineteenth century.

No coal ever came out of the Pelsall mine again. All the equipment has been removed, every item cleaned and repaired ready to be sold off at auction. While none of the mining equipment, not even ropes, remain underground, the body of William Richards, the twenty-second man to be killed that day, remains entombed underground.

One shaft, known as No. 8, had been backfilled after closure in the 1930s but four decades later the infill collapsed. By then the land around had been built on, and what had been the shaft suddenly reopened at the corner of Wolverhampton Road and School Lane.

Now the responsibility of the National Coal Board, both No. 8 and its companion No. 9 were refilled, grouted, and capped to comply with later regulations.

On 14 December 1887, No. 9 shaft had also seen an explosion. This was the result of the great pressure building up after the winding operation had been completed. Damage proved minimal, but it did dislodge a brick from the lining of the shaft, which had landed on a miner's leg and broke it. The leg, which had been the wooden leg of a man in the shaft, was soon replaced. Made from the handle of an old pick helve, he wore it on the way home. The 'broken' part of the leg is still thought to be lying somewhere underground, although probably rotted away over a century later.

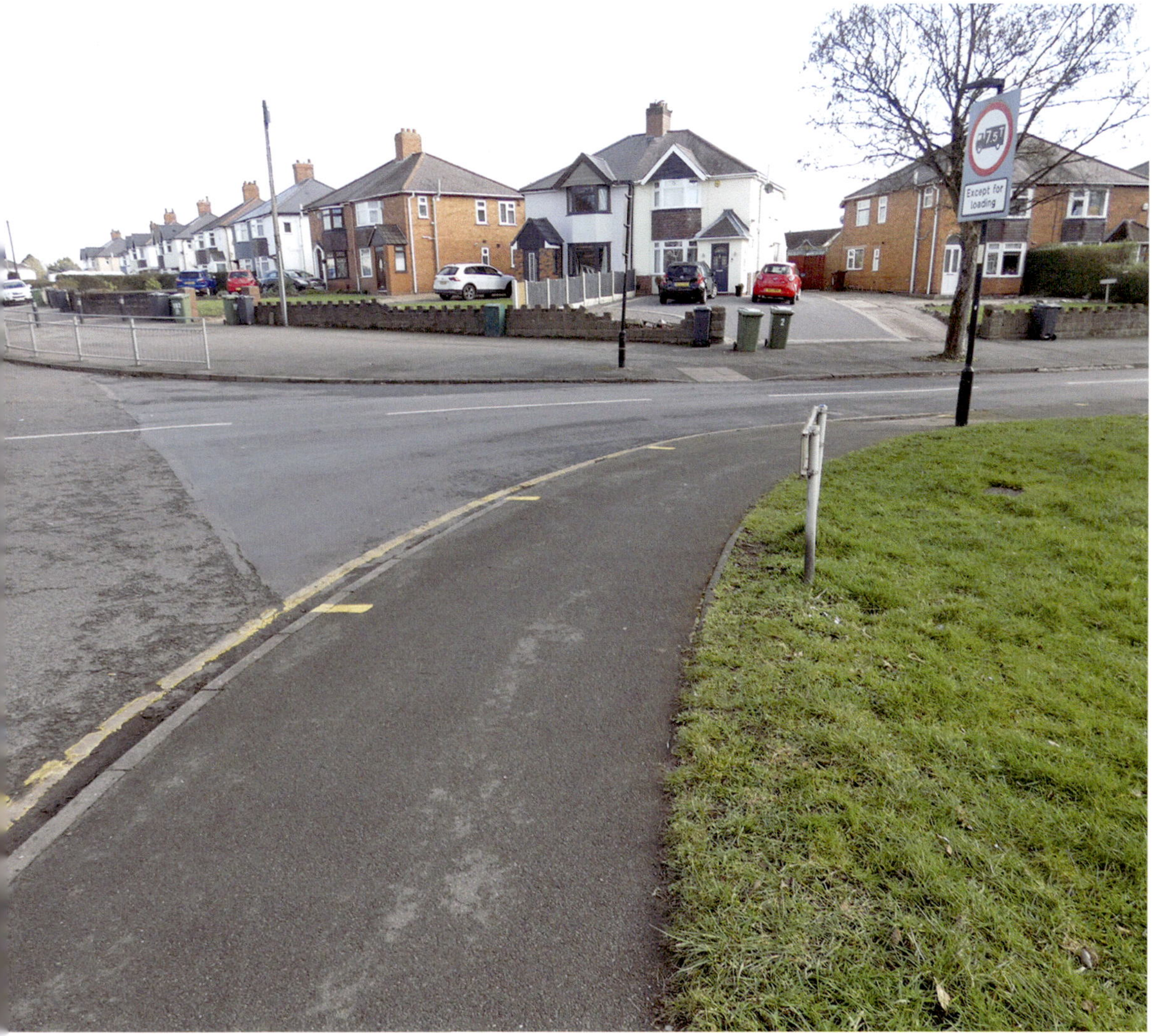

Where the ground collapsed in the 1970s at Wolverhampton Road and School Lane.

23

THE CROOKED HOUSE

With the previous chapters all looking at closed mine workings, and these quite clearly unreachable in the modern era, it became clear something visible should be offered to show the many miles of tunnels do sometimes manifest themselves above ground.

Undoubtedly the workings have influenced the land above, not least in the release of potentially dangerous gases. Note the references to capping shafts in previous chapters are as much to prevent gases, and other unwanted effluents, from seeping from the old mine workings as much as preventing anyone from falling down the shafts. While there are several examples we could have looked at, perhaps the most obvious and accessible evidence, can be found at the aptly named Crooked House public house.

Formerly located on the Himley Road on the former Coppice Mill site, this had been built as a farmhouse in 1765. Originally part of the Oak Farm Estate as Oak Farm Mill, the region came into the ownership of the Glynne family by marriage in the latter part of the eighteenth century. In 1835 the farm was turned over for the mining of iron and clay, as well as coal. Industrial activity ceased in 1875, following the death of Sir Stephen Glynne (brother-in-law of Liberal Prime Minister William Ewart Gladstone), with all the equipment removed and sold off – this made sense as mining continued in the area and the family wanted to recoup something from their mining operations.

With the closure of the mine, the premises, which had been known as the Siden House since 1830 became the Glynne Arms. The resulting mining subsidence created the distinctive appearance of the building and, while originally condemned as unsafe, steps were eventually taken to shore up the building and create a unique experience for customers by Wolverhampton and Dudley Breweries using a series of buttresses and girders. The subsidence produces some strange effects, this includes seeing items apparently roll uphill, this merely an optical illusion but still quite disorienting. While the brewery took advantage to relaunch the public house with a new name, the Crooked House, they could simply have gone back to the original name of Siden House, for 'siden' is a local dialect word meaning 'crooked'. Only one side of the building was sinking, the lean a little over 4 feet from the vertical.

In 2023 the building was sold and swiftly afterwards gutted by a fire and ultimately demolished. The owners were charged with arson and issued an order to rebuild the pub, lean and all.

24

HAMSTEAD COLLIERY

For many of us the image of a coal mine, at least that part found beneath the surface, is very simple indeed. In its most basic form, it is comprised of a single shaft dropping down to the coal seam or seams, thereafter the seams are dug out leaving tunnels, shored up to make them safe. This is ostensibly what we do find, albeit not quite as simple.

Firstly, it is very unusual to find a coal seam lying horizontally. While they will have been laid down this way, movement of the Earth's crust has tilted, folded, and faulted the seams over millions of years. Furthermore, it clearly makes more sense to sink a second or even a third shaft rather than transport coal over lengthy distance to haul it to the surface. When we consider these extra shafts could well be sunk decades apart and some, as we have seen in an earlier chapter, were unrecorded and thus unknown until eventually linking up with later workings. Also taking into consideration the many changes in ownership, and even mining methods, the old workings beneath the surface are a lot more complex than we realise.

Even when taking these factors into consideration, Hamstead Colliery has excelled itself when it comes to changes over the near century of mining. Formed in April 1875, the newly founded Hamstead Colliery Company acquired land from the Calthorpe family at Perry Hall, sinking their first shafts the following year. Not until 1878 was the first coal extracted, the delay due to unexpected problems with the geology, water coming into the workings, and not least the depth of the coal seam – 2,000 feet down, making it the deepest coal mine in the world at one point.

Within twenty years the mine had closed. Fire in the deepest part of the mine proved impossible to control and the company closed the mine, ending the employ of 800. Yet within two years, and the region suffering from a severe coal shortage, the mine opened again. Not only did change occur below ground but also above, where a redrawing of boundaries in 1928 meant the colliery officially became part of West Bromwich, then in 1974 county boundary changes took the mine out of Staffordshire and placed it in the West Midlands.

Undoubtedly, the worst moment in Hamstead Colliery's history came on Wednesday 4 March 1908, although problems had begun the previous week when an accident meant the mine had not been operating at full capacity. Had it done so, perhaps the fire might have been noted and the subsequent disaster avoided, or maybe more may have been trapped that day. When news of the fire 1,800 feet down reached the surface, thirty-nine individuals were still trapped. Fourteen of these managed to escape to the surface, and a rescue attempt quickly launched. Local rescue parties were beaten back by the thick smoke, and little progress made until two rescue teams arrived from Yorkshire, complete

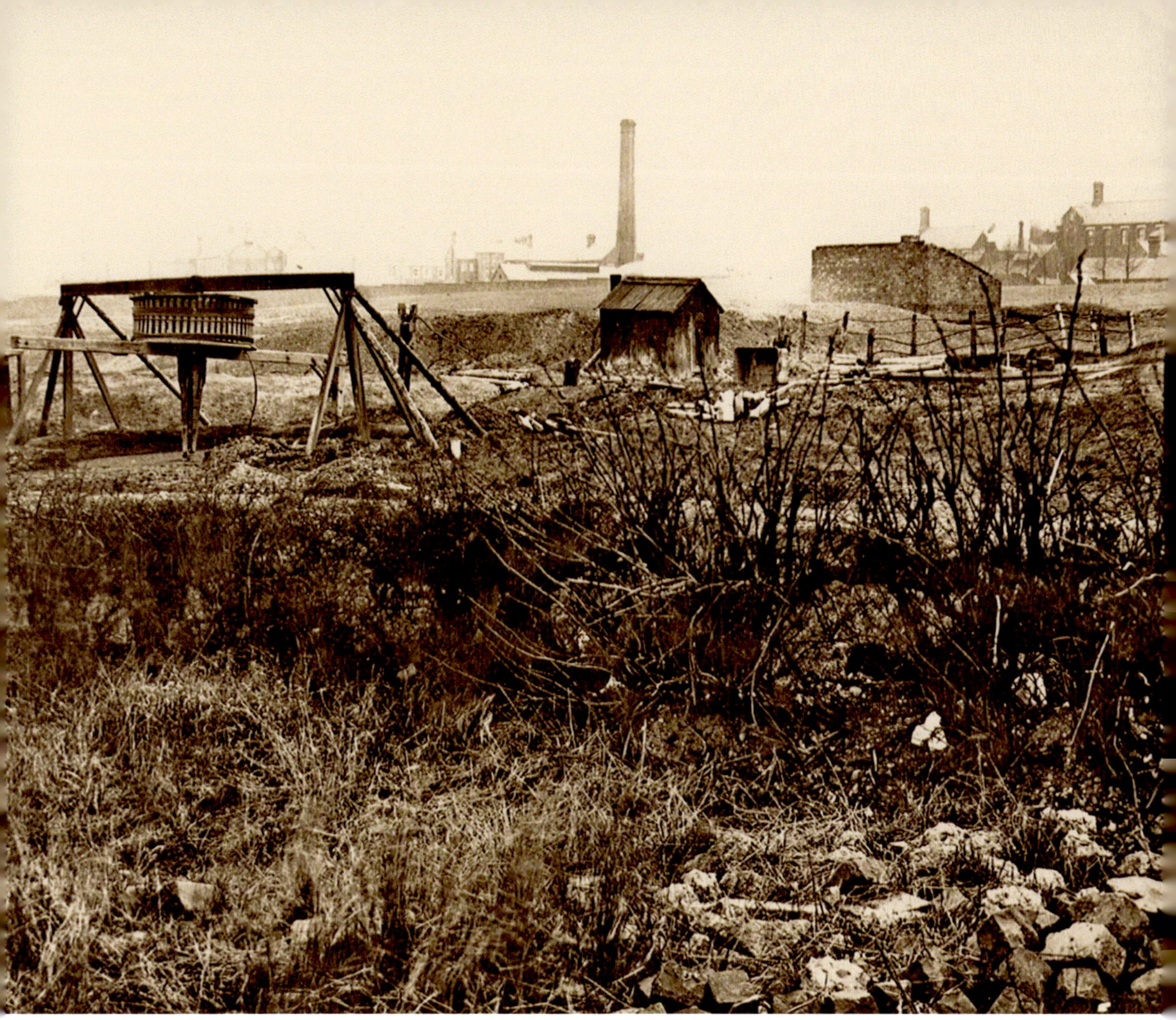

This site appears to have been abandoned, but the gin, the wooden framework and the corrugated-iron outbuildings can clearly be seen. There is also a clear view of the workhouse (now Burton Road Hospital) on the right. A rough track can also clearly be seen to the right, which may have been used for coal or equipment transportation. (Ref: p/1848, courtesy of Dudley Archives and Local History Service)

with breathing apparatus. Even then one rescue party ran into trouble and had trouble reaching the surface, indeed one rescuer suffered from heatstroke and John Welsby became the first confirmed victim. Hope for the others grew when they found a tabby cat alive and well in the shaft, but this optimism proved short-lived.

It took until the following week to extinguish the fire, ventilate the mine, and find the missing men. They found their twenty-five colleagues in four groups, one of which had left their thoughts on a message board. The brief chalk-written note read 'The Lord Preserve Us.' Twenty-eight pit ponies were also found dead. Last to be retrieved the body of John Welsby, he posthumously awarded the Edward VII medal and has a road named after him, fittingly located where the mine once stood. A century after the disaster, a memorial bearing the names of the twenty-six who died was erected. It takes the form of a coal tub on rails, mounted on a brick plinth.

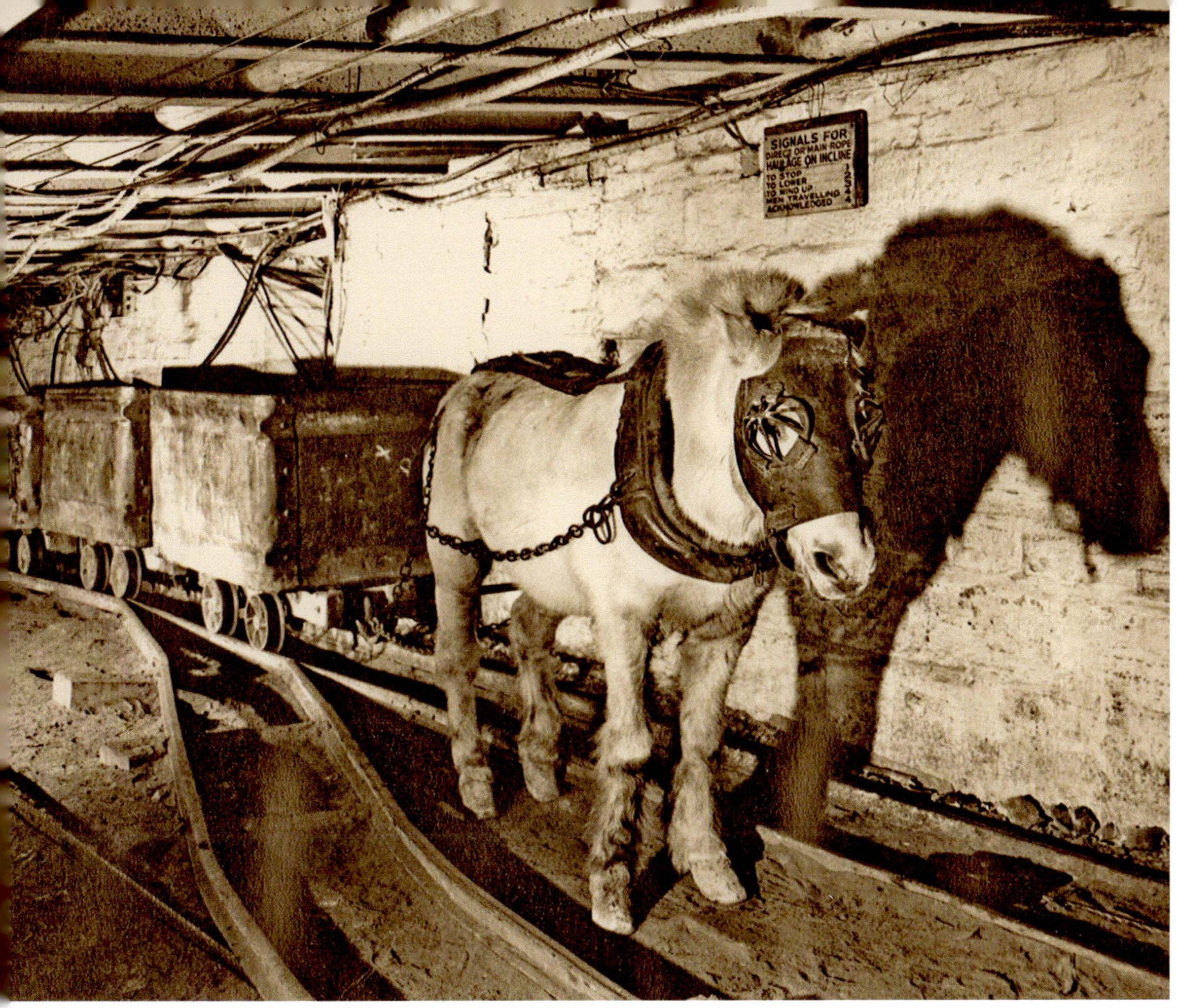

A pit pony hauling coal tubs at Warwick Colliery in the Black Country. The horse is wearing protective head gear. There appear to be electric cables along the ceiling and walls which helps to date the photograph as perhaps being late twentieth century. Note the sign on the wall advising on signals used for hauling tubs up and down the slope (maybe using the rope in the bottom left-hand corner of the photograph). The numbers suggest the number of bangs or bumps (or anything that could be heard) needed for a particular action. (Ref: p/1997, courtesy of Dudley Archives and Local History Service)

25

SANDWELL PARK JUBILEE COLLIERY

As with the look at the Crooked House, this colliery and its workings are revealed by subsidence. However, rather than a single narrative, this place has had a succession of tales to tell from its long and varied history.

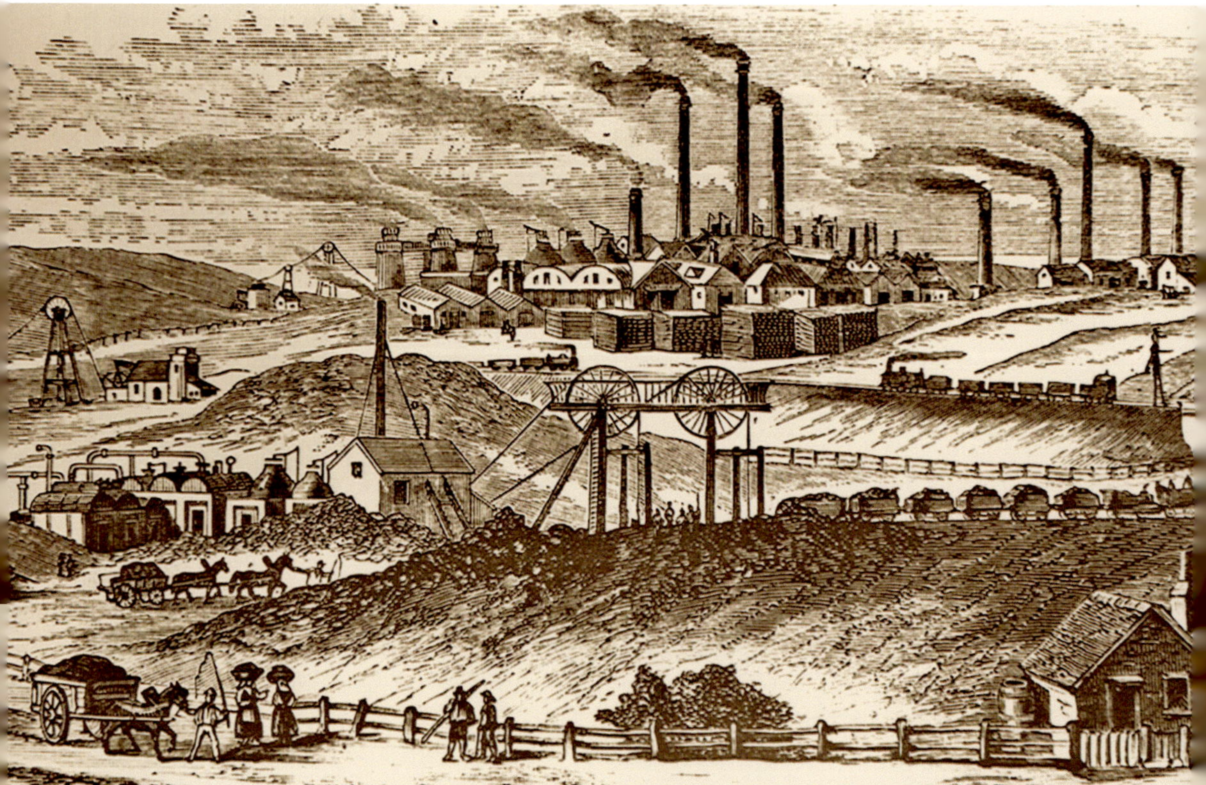

A photograph of an etched drawing showing two of the Earl of Dudley's thick coal pits in the Black Country region. The image is somewhat stylised, particularly with regard to the figures in the picture, and possibly does not reflect the harsh environmental conditions that the coal-mining industry produced. (Ref: p/1820, courtesy of Dudley Archives and Local History Service)

Our earliest record of the region comes from the archives of Sandwell Priory. Their records speak of this twelfth century Benedictine monastery being established on the site of a former hermitage, although we have no idea how long such had been here. That monastery closed in 1525, on the orders of Cardinal Wolsey, and by the first years of the eighteenth century, Sandwell Hall stood here. Built as the home of the Earl of Dartmouth, the hall had also been used as an asylum in the late nineteenth century, in 1907 it is listed as Sandwell Hall Industrial School for Mentally Defective Boys, then in 1928 the hall was demolished owing to subsidence. The cause for the troubles being the Sandwell Hall Jubilee Colliery, where more than 600 miners earned a living.

During the 1960s the site was redeveloped again, this time as Sandwell Valley Country Park. Its 660 acres have been set aside as a wildlife area and leisure facility. It includes Forge Mill Lake, a region which is set for further remodelling, as part of a flood risk management scheme. We can only guess at how much water has and will be removed from the site through the empty tunnels and shafts lying below, at least those still in existence.

26

WOLVERHAMPTON CANAL TUNNEL

Found on the Birmingham Main Line Canal just to the south of Wolverhampton Railway Station, this is often referred to as the Broad Street Bridge. Being on the Birmingham Main Line Canal and with Birmingham's Broad Street connections to the canal much better known, such a reference is asking for confusion. Correctly, as the title of the chapter shows, this is the Wolverhampton Canal Tunnel and is wide enough to allow two boats to pass beneath it with ease.

Nearly 100 yards in length, there can be no argument that this is indeed a tunnel. That the tunnel has a distinctive arch also helps to convince us it is a tunnel. Indeed, there is no argument as to whether this is a tunnel – although there remains the oft-quoted wrong name of Broad Street Bridge (and there is no doubting this is not a bridge). Yet this does raise the question asked in the early chapters of just what is a tunnel?

If the answer is that the longest boat should be completely contained at any one moment within the structure, then this is undoubtedly a tunnel. This then raises a question just 250 yards north of the Wolverhampton Canal Tunnel, where the Wednesbury Road crosses the same canal, as to why this is considered a bridge and not a tunnel. It is certainly long enough to contain the full length of the boat, but perhaps the answer lies in there not being the distinctive arch associated with tunnelling. If the lack of an arch is the clue, then this suggests the thought is that a tunnel has to be bored through, but that is rarely the case and many canals and railway 'tunnels' are created by the cut and cover method, just as the Wolverhampton Canal Tunnel clearly has. As the Wednesbury Road 'bridge' clearly encloses the canal and any boats and has been created by building a route above, it would take a strong argument to show this is not the second or perhaps the New Wolverhampton Canal Tunnel.

27

WOLVERHAMPTON LOW LEVEL RAILWAY

Wolverhampton Low Level Railway Line opened in 1854, although not known as such until 1856. Initially operating on the Great Western Railway wide gauge, standard gauge came in 1869. Although the Wolverhampton Low Level Station closed in 1959, the line saw a considerable increase in traffic between 1963 and 1967 owing t the electrification of the High Level route. By 1967, only the Birmingham Snow Hill to Wednesbury Central trains came along the Low Level line, and all traffic ceased in 1972.

Much of the tracks were left in situ in the hope that a service may be restored. That happened in 1999 with the coming of the Midland Metro Railway, but this line turns away along the A41 Bilston Road before reaching the Low Level. Much redevelopment of the Low Level Station site over the years has reduced signs of the underground tunnels greatly, yet we can still see the portals which lead under Wolverhampton.

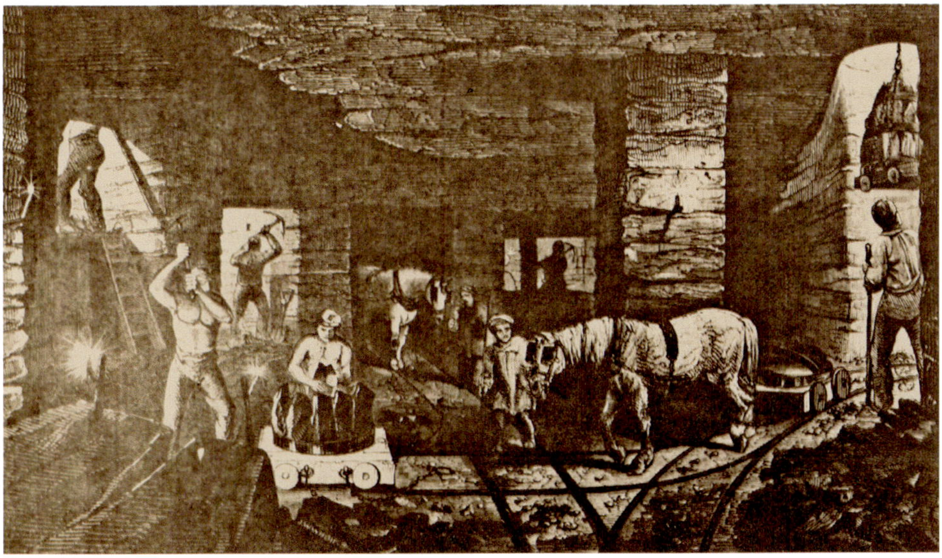

Photograph of an illustration showing miners digging the ten-yard coal with pickaxes in the part of the mine where the coal is thickest. Note the use of rushlights for lighting as opposed to candles or lamps for lighting. The miner on the right appears to be sorting through the coal before placing it on the wheeled trolley to be transported out of the mine on tracks, before then being hauled up to the surface in cages. Note also the use of horses for transportation. (Ref: p/1825, courtesy of Dudley Archives and Local History Service)

Standing on Lower Walsall Street looking north, with Corser Street to the right and the High Level Lines to the left, we can see what looks for all the world like an abandoned canal. Peering through the fence and ahead we can clearly see two portals which, with the blue bricks of the wall and tunnel ends, clearly reveal this as the former entrance to tunnel leading to Wolverhampton Low Level Railway Station. Here we are looking at the 'Up', to the left, and the 'Down', to the right, lines running for 377 yards under Wolverhampton.

And this is not the only disused underground feature here, for a subway constructed between the High Level and Low Level stations is still in existence. Its white-glazed brickwork and decorative iron railings show this had not been designed as any temporary measure. Known as the Colonnades, it is a Grade II listed structure, and at the time of writing is closed.

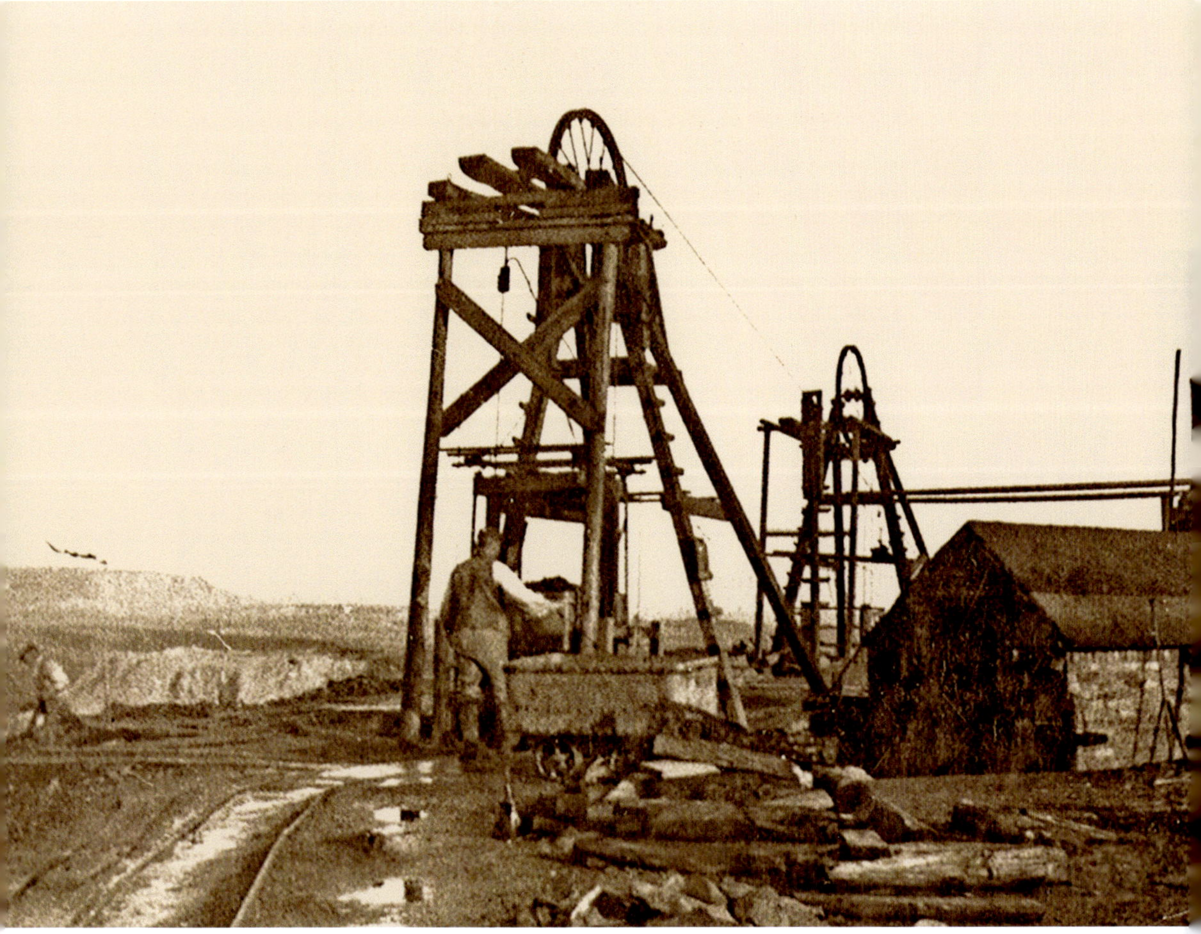

This image shows the typical wooden pithead gear and coal truck. The miner in the centre of the picture appears to be tending a truck loaded with coal that has just emerged from the coal shaft. The pile of wooden planks in the foreground may have been used for pit props underground. (Ref: p/1864, courtesy of Dudley Archives and Local History Service)

28

BLACK LAKE TUNNEL

Black Lake Tunnel carries the railway line between West Bromwich and Wednesbury. Built by the Great Western Railway for the line between Birmingham Snow Hill and Wolverhampton Low Level stations, the 412 yards are still in use by the Midland Metro, albeit that line only runs to one side and is only lit on that side of the tunnel. At the northern portal the road running parallel to it is, appropriately known as Tunnel Road.

The south end of Tunnel Road. (Richard Vince, CC BY-SA 2.0)

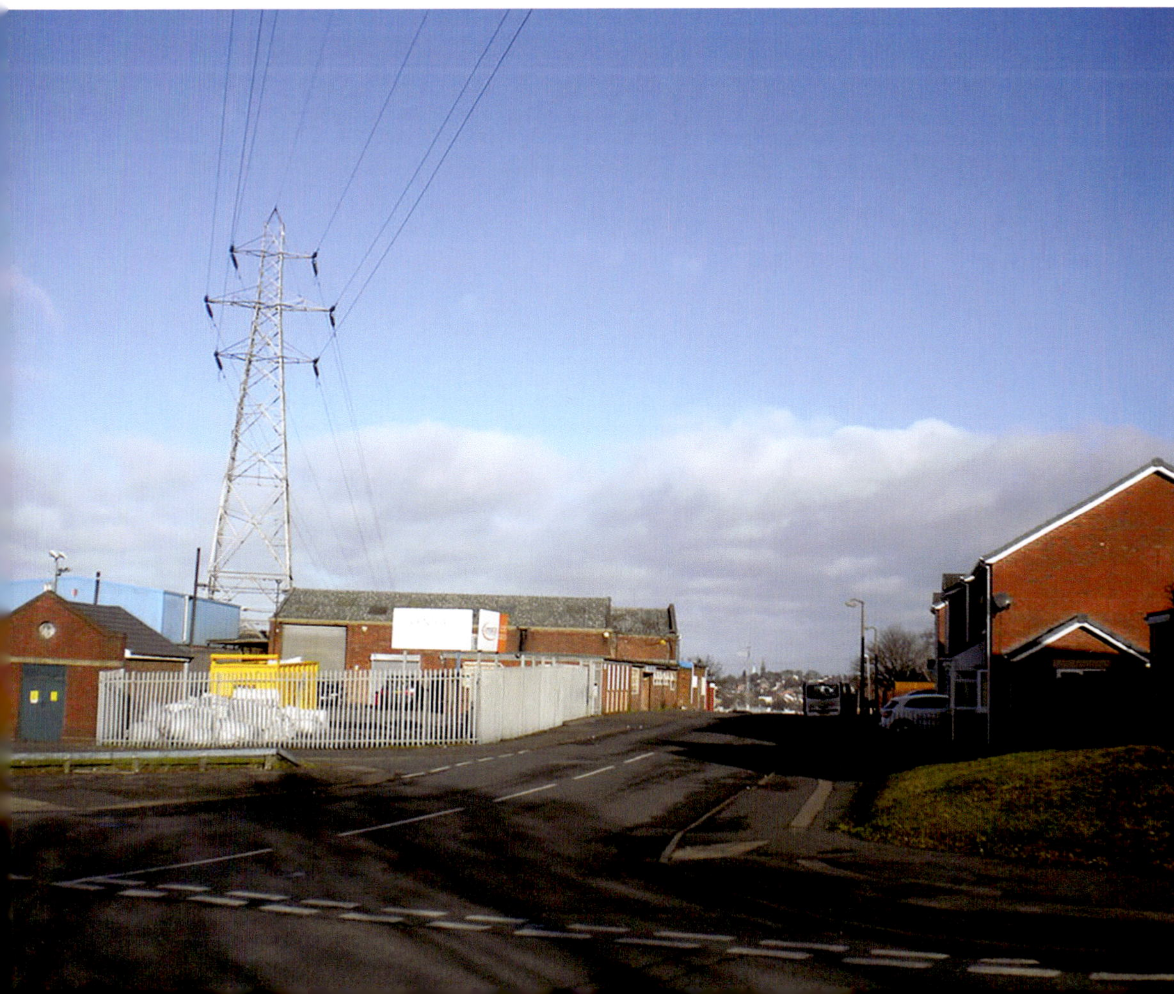

29

TIPTON TUNNEL

We have had tunnels for canals and for railways. Now, at last, we have one for a road. Taking two years to construct and costing more than £22 million, the tunnel ended years of traffic misery by bringing the road under the West Coast Mainline. Prior to opening the 190-foot tunnel, Owen Street traffic had to negotiate a level crossing where the barriers were lowered for as much as forty-five minutes in every hour. The road does not follow the same line as that leading to the level crossing, and the improvements included work to Tipton Station car park, a canal bridge, and pedestrian access.

Construction work on Tipton Tunnel, 2009. (Michael Clark, CC BY 2.0)

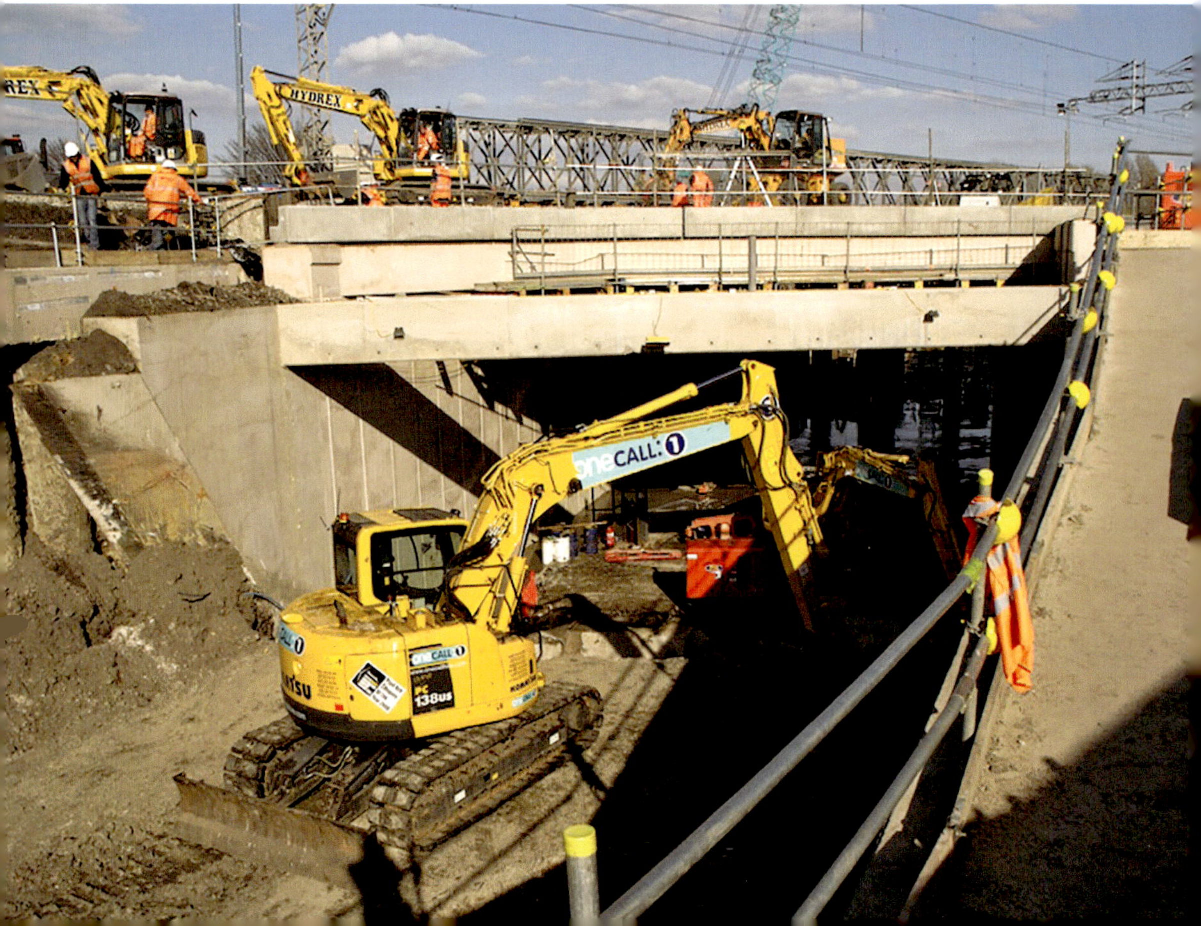

30

WALSALL STATION TUNNEL

Walsall Station boasts a tunnel, or does it? Some argue this is not a tunnel but simply a lower-level track which has been built over, leaving room for trains to run below. But with the rails hidden from above between St Paul's Street in the northeast to emerge alongside the Saddlers Shopping Centre and the ends of the platforms soon after, does this not function as a tunnel and is therefore underground? Who is to say whether a tunnel has to be excavated through the ground, or simply dug out and covered over?

Whether this is a tunnel or not, it is included because, at least in the modern day, it is underground. That fact is undeniable and can be seen in the nation's capital, the first city in the world to build and operate an underground railway. In early days tunnelling was the method of construction but, with problems soon revealing themselves – collapses the more obvious hold-up, but the removal of material from a tunnel under construction can only be in the one direction. Thus, for the earliest shallow underground railways, engineers soon turned to the cut and cover method. In this method a trench is dug, albeit a large trench, the rails and infrastructure added, then the whole is covered. Thereafter the street, with its traffic and pedestrians, continues as before. No tunnelling, and yet nobody would argue the London Underground does not run underground for much of its routes.

Walsall station tunnel under Saddlers Shopping Centre. (Elliott Brown, CC BY 2.0)

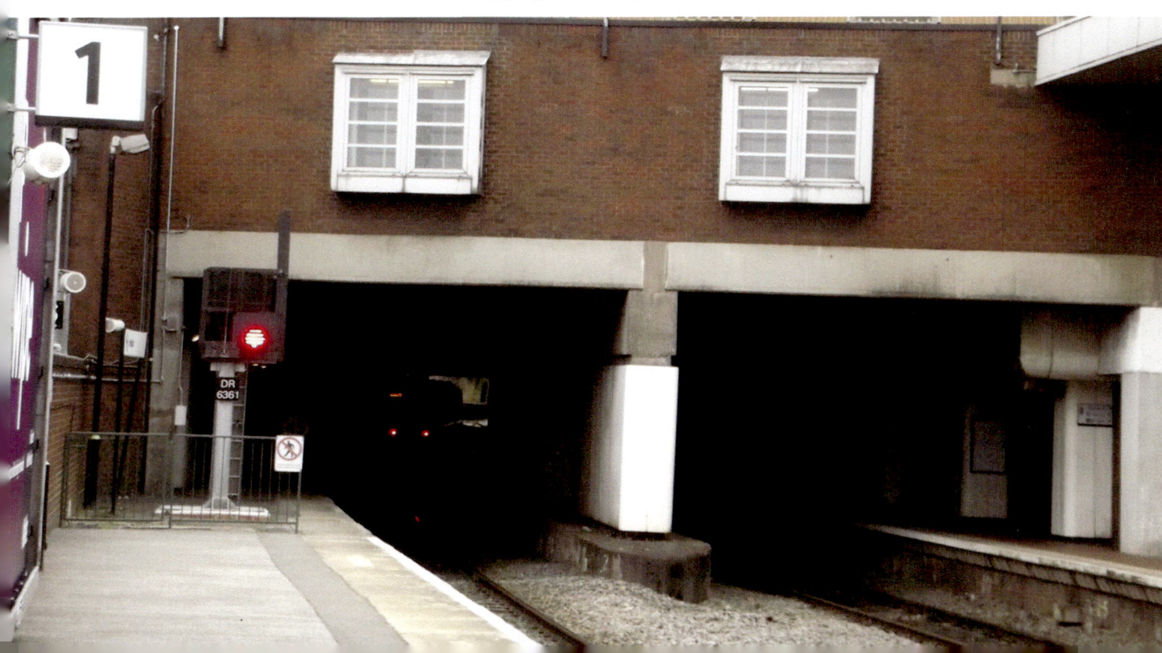

31

HEATH TOWN RAILWAY TUNNEL

Heath Town in Wolverhampton has a railway tunnel on the Grand Junction line. Disappearing underground at the junction of Tudor Road and Wolverhampton Road, the line runs east beneath the Wolverhampton Road and the canal (and also a National Cycleway route). A short tunnel indeed, but a tunnel it is.

Heath Town railway tunnel. (John M., CC BY-SA 2.0)

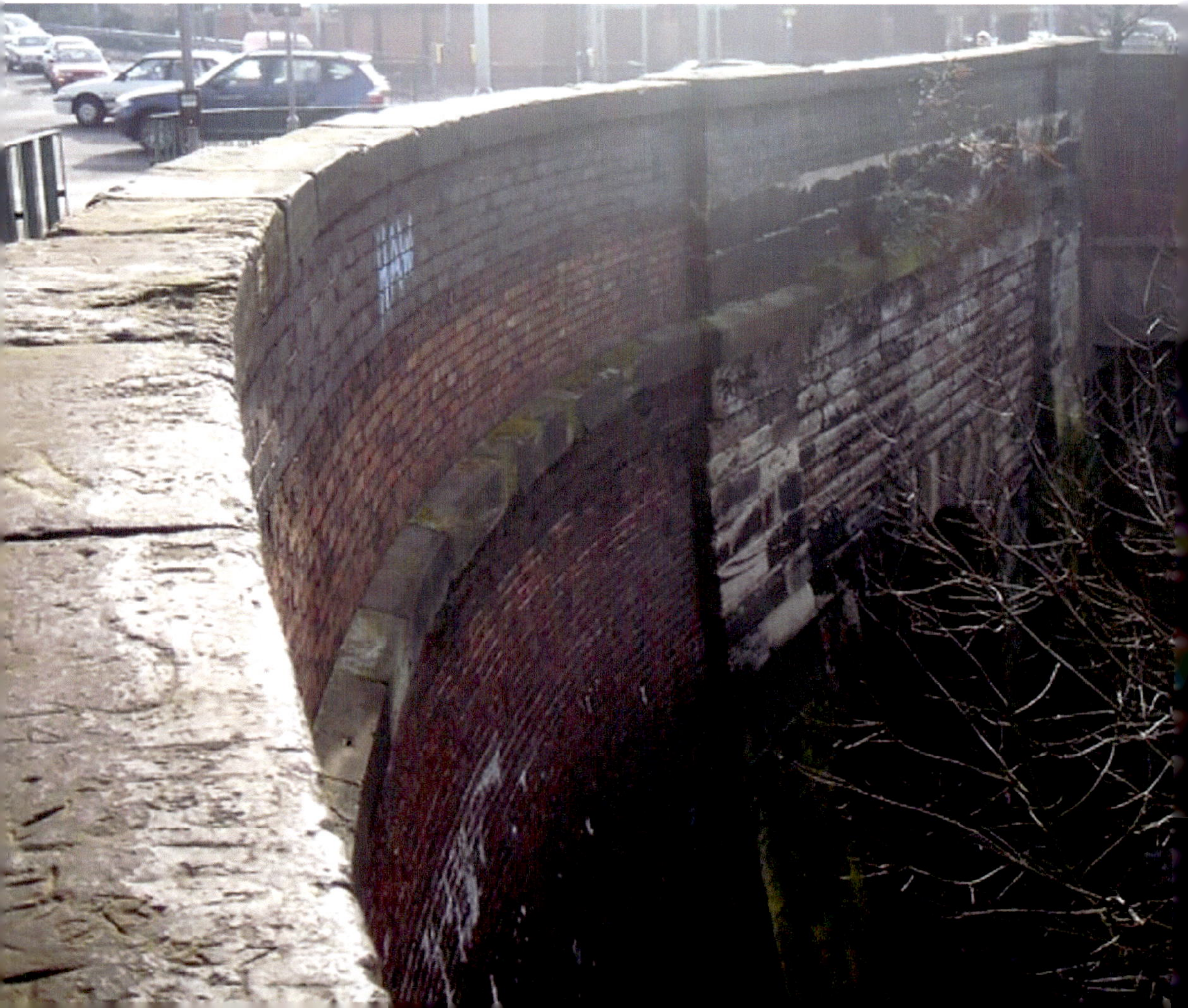

32

FENS BRANCH CANAL TUNNEL

The Fens Branch Canal tunnel, once described as the Stourbridge Canal, has been completely covered by a modern housing estate. However, the entrance portal is clearly visible. By matching an old map to the modern version, it is clear this short stretch of tunnel ran from the present-day canal in the west, to emerge at a point where Cressett Avenue meets Cressett Lane at Brierley Hill.

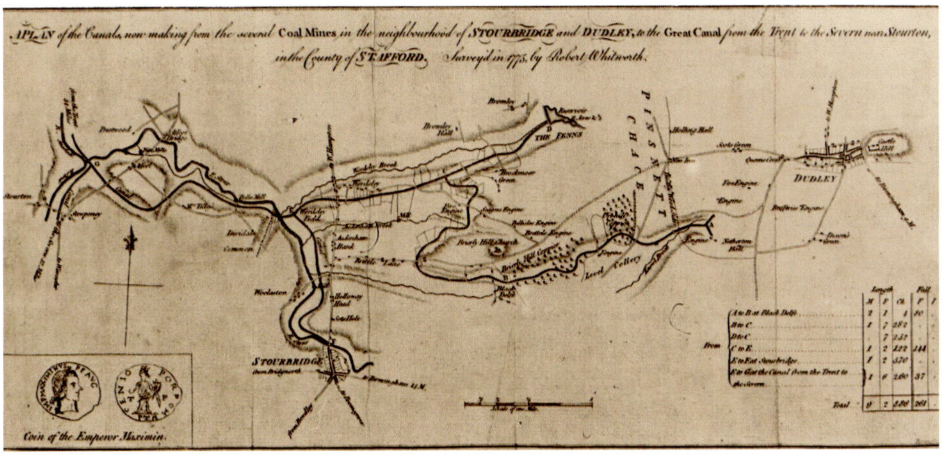

A plan of the canals from the several coal mines in the region of Stourbridge and Dudley to the Great Canal from the Trent to the Severn near Stourton, in Stafford. Surveyed in 1775 by Robert Whitworth. (Ref: p7/1201, courtesy of Dudley Archives and Local History Service)

BIBLIOGRAPHY

Bills, D. M. and E and W. R. Griffiths, *Kinver Rock Houses*

Boynton, John, *Rails Through the Hills*

Burne, S. A. H. and M. J. Wise, *Roads and Canals in Staffordshire*

Cannock Chase Mining Historical Society, *The Cannock Chase Coalfield and its Coal Mines*

Collins, Paul, *Black Country Canals*

Doherty, Andrew, *Rail Around Birmingham: The Black Country and South Staffordshire*

Dunphy, Angus, *A Geography of the Parishes of Wombourne and Lower Penn*

Hadfield, Charles, *The Canals of the West Midlands*

Langford, J. Ian, *Stourbridge Canal*

Poulton-Smith, Anthony, *Black Country Ghosts*

Vodden, David F., *Our Black Country*